Principles into Practice
in Early Childhood Education

Principles into Practice in Early Childhood Education

Edited by
G.M. Blenkin and A.V. Kelly

P·C·P
Paul Chapman
Publishing Ltd

Copyright © 1997, Geva M. Blenkin and A.V. Kelly.

Paul Chapman Publishing Ltd
144 Liverpool Road
London
N1 1LA

British Library Cataloguing in Publication Data

Principles into practice in early childhood education
   1. Elementary school teachers – Certification   2. Elementary
   school teachers – Attitudes
   I. Blenkin, Geva M.   II. Kelly, A. V. (Albert Victor), 1931–
   372.1'12

ISBN 1 85396 306 2

Typeset by Dorwyn Ltd, Rowlands Castle, Hants
Printed and bound in Great Britain

A B C D E F G H   9 8 7

Contents

Preface

This book offers a report on the main findings of research conducted during the first phase of a major project, 'Principles into Practice: Improving the Quality of Children's Early Learning'. The project begins from a commitment to the view that the major determinant of quality of provision is the expertise of the early years practitioner. And so the project, which is designed in three phases, aims to investigate the ways in which early learning in group settings can be improved by raising the quality of the practice of those professionals who work with young children.

The research team recognized at the outset, however, that, in order to promote the professional development of practitioners, it was necessary to gain a clear picture of the realities of existing provision. During the first phase of the project, therefore, a major part of the research activity was directed at conducting an extensive survey of current provision for young children (from birth to 8 years of age) in England and Wales.

In surveying this range of provision, the research team has sought to obtain information concerning both the nature and the quality of provision, particularly by exploring such major determinants of quality as the settings in which provision is made, the level of resourcing and the qualifications of those professionals and others who are working with young children. In keeping with the project's commitment to the importance of professional practice, the data also have a qualitative dimension in that the survey set out to elicit the views of practitioners on what might constitute quality of provision for early learning. These views were explored in greater detail through a series of structured interviews conducted with the heads of a small selection of early years settings in the south east of England. Full details of the approach we adopted to the research are set out in Chapter 1.

The national survey has yielded a remarkably rich pool of data, and the first aim of this report is to present its main findings. These are drawn both from the quantitative data, relating to practitioners' qualifications and training and the nature of the early years settings, and from a qualitative analysis of the practitioners' views of those factors which support and constrain a quality curriculum for the early years. This is the focus of Chapters 2 and 3 of the book.

A second aim is to amplify the analysis by drawing upon the narrative data from both the national survey and the structured interviews. This narrative analysis is undertaken in Chapter 4, which sets out to explore the stories practitioners told about quality and the early years curriculum. It aims to deepen our understanding of these stories, by seeking to reveal their complex meanings.

The third aim of this book is to describe our preparation for the Second Phase of the project's work, which is the extension of our findings, both quantitative and qualitative, into professional development through action research. This preparation has consisted of an exploration of the effectiveness of action research as a device for supporting professional development through a series of pilot studies undertaken in selected early years settings. This is the substance of Chapter 5.

The book is, therefore, an account of the first contribution from this project towards the debate about improving the quality of children's early learning. The developmental activities it has generated, which are the focus of the action research procedures of Phase Two, will be reported in a subsequent publication.

Acknowledgements

The research team wishes to acknowledge the generous financial support provided by the Esmée Fairbairn Charitable Trust, not only for Phase One of the project, whose findings are recorded here, but also for the research and development work of Phase Two which will be the subject of a further publication.

Our thanks are also due to the members of the Steering Committee whose help has been invaluable to us in providing both expert guidance and continuous moral support.

The research team: Phase One

Geva M. Blenkin	–	*Director*
Marian Whitehead	–	*Deputy Director (School Settings)*
Victoria Hurst	–	*Deputy Director (Preschool Settings)*
Norah Yue	–	*Research Associate*
Janet Rose	–	*Action Researcher*
Gwyn Edwards	–	*Research Partner*
Vic Kelly	–	*Chairperson, Project Steering Committee*

Introduction

'In all things the beginning is the most important part.' So declared Plato, in relation to early education, more than two millennia ago. The truth of this assertion is recognized in almost every area of experience. The foundations of a building are acknowledged as crucial to the fully developed structure; the keel of a ship as critical to its stability; the appropriate nurture of the seedling as essential to its future growth. And, since the introduction of state-maintained education for children in the early years, effective provision at this stage has been seen as central to future success – an intuition which has recently been substantiated by extensive research evidence.

Furthermore, in all fields, it has been recognized that the beginnings also require different kinds of approach and provision from the later stages, and perhaps more care and consideration. Once the foundations have been properly laid, the building activity can proceed apace; once the keel is laid down, the construction and fitting out of the vessel are relatively straightforward processes; once the seedlings have been fostered, the plants can be left to grow with minimal attention. And, similarly, the education of the very young needs to be approached in a different way, and certainly needs an important admixture of care, if it is to provide a sound foundation for future development – social, personal and moral as well as academic and intellectual.

Thus the planning of educational provision for the early years must not only be recognized as pivotal in relation to later development, it must also be seen as requiring a different approach, a different set of planning – and evaluative – criteria; it must have 'its own canons of excellence and criteria of success', as the Hadow Report (Board of Education, 1931, p. xxii) said of primary education as a whole. Further, as that report went on to add, 'it must have the courage to stand by them'.

The research described in this book, which comes from the First Phase of the project, 'Principles into Practice: Improving the Quality of

Children's Early Learning' (PiP), has set out to identify what these canons of excellence and criteria of success might be. We have approached this task by, first, attempting to establish the real views and values of the practitioners themselves. This is in line with that conviction of the centrality of the practitioner to quality provision which we declared in our Preface, which in turn derives from the evidence of much research into curriculum change and development, which has revealed most starkly that 'all curriculum development is teacher [or practitioner] development'.

The research has been undertaken in response to the growing recognition, throughout modern societies, of the importance of early childhood education. This recognition owes a great deal to the research which has already been carried out, especially in the USA, and which has revealed the long-lasting and life-enhancing effects of good-quality early educational provision. And it is reflected in the newly acquired high profile of this sector of educational provision in the policies of all major political parties in the UK, and in the avowed intention of all of them to increase the availability of such provision.

What is too often overlooked, however, in what is both said and done for early childhood education is that the research has revealed not that such provision of itself is beneficial but that benefits only accrue when that provision is of a high quality. Young children gain few advantages, beyond the obvious, from being cared for in institutions or other contexts in which their safety and security, important as these are, are the sole or prime concerns. To gain educationally, to enjoy those experiences which have been shown to lead to more satisfactory forms of personal and social adjustment, they need to be placed in situations and provided with facilities which will positively foster such development.

Hence three things need to be done and need to be done with some urgency. First, we need a clearer picture of current provision in all its complexities in order to evaluate its effectiveness. Second, we need a more detailed analysis of what constitutes a defensible definition of quality provision at this stage of educational development. And, third, we need to devise strategies which will help us to raise the quality of existing provision so that it more nearly matches the criteria of quality identified. These are the three tasks which this research has sought to address.

The first stage of this research, therefore, was a national survey of existing provision for early education in all forms of group-setting throughout England and Wales. In general, that survey has revealed that existing provision leaves much to be desired on any kind of definition of quality. It also – more disturbingly – reveals that current trends, deriving from current political policies, are leading towards a deterioration rather than an enhancement of quality of provision.

This is one reason why a clearer definition of quality is needed. The second dimension of the research, therefore, has been to seek for such a definition, at least a definition accepted by those who might be seen as the most experienced professionals working in the field (the heads of institutions), as part of that national survey. Thus all respondents were asked not merely to give factual details of the nature of their provision, but also to identify what they saw as barriers to quality in that provision and to indicate what they regarded as the major constituents of high quality. It is here that the evidence of current inadequacies, as perceived by the practitioners themselves, is most strong.

As will be seen later from the account of our findings, what emerged from this survey as the most prominent and significant determinant of quality was, as we have indicated we expected, the ability and competence of the practitioners, the adults in the equation, whether these are teachers, nursery nurses, qualified carers or simply people who generously give their time and energies to the care of the very young. Stage three of the research, therefore, has focused on the development of strategies for professional development, devices for raising the levels of competence and improving the professional skills of the practitioners. The major strategy adopted to achieve this has been that of action research. This work is still at an early stage. Some initial reflections on its effectiveness are offered in Chapter 5, and a follow-up publication is planned which will provide a more detailed account and analysis of this stage of the project, and highlight its implications for the professional development of early years practitioners.

It will be seen from this that the project team has set itself a series of tasks which embrace both research and development and which thus require both quantitative and qualitative analyses.

A major reason for this has been an awareness of the practical and professional inadequacy of much so-called research in education. For too often such research, while perhaps of great interest to members of the research community, has had little relevance for, and thus little impact on, the realities of educational practice. The theory/practice gap has not been bridged. Indeed, it is not difficult to identify examples of educational research which has been positively counterproductive to the advancement of professional practice by identifying weaknesses in the work of practioners without offering guidance towards viable alternatives, a process which has diminished rather than enhanced confidence and thus, with it, practical competence.

The body which has so far funded this research project, however, the Esmée Fairbairn Charitable Trust, made it a requirement that any research undertaken should be of a kind and adopt a form which would significantly influence practice. Quite rightly, therefore, it has looked for dissemination on as wide a national scale as possible – to people working directly with children in the early years and the children's families, as well as to academics, policy-makers and trainers. And this was a requirement to which we were only too ready and willing to respond.

The concern of this project team, then, has been to try to bridge that theory/practice gap, not merely to identify inadequacies but to devise effective strategies for tackling them. And, to achieve this, it is necessary for any research to get beyond the acquisition of merely empirical and quantitative data and to provide a qualitative analysis on the basis of which policy-makers and practitioners can make those decisions of value which must lie at the heart of any genuinely educational provision.

The team has thus had to devise research methodologies which would meet the several inter-related but very different – even conceptually different – tasks which it set itself. The focus has had to be not merely on research *and* development but on research *with* development or development *through* research. And that development has had to be shown to be founded on solid research data of a qualitative kind.

Thus, the research began with a conventional analysis of the quantitative data, designed to reveal the realities of current provision. In particular, we were concerned to discover more about the quantity and nature of the qualifications and experience of practitioners working with young children. In addition to the training patterns, however, we needed to know more about the quality of the provision being made.

A major strategy which has been adopted for achieving this has been the use of narrative analysis of the qualitative data, collected from the national survey and other sources, particularly the structured interviews. For this has been seen as the only device by which the messages, the 'stories', of those qualitative data can be elicited, made public and given status in both research and development terms.

As we indicated in our Preface, we started from the assumption that the quality of the practitioner is the most important factor in ensuring quality of provision. And, as will be seen, this has been confirmed by the research itself. Improving the quality of provision, therefore, must begin with the professional development of the practitioners. To achieve this, we need not only to know more about the training and the experience of the practitioners but also to gain a clearer picture of what they value and consider to be essential for the care and education of young children. The empirical information is of value in guiding policy-makers in the making of appropriate provision; the qualitative data, however, provide those responsible for professional development, including crucially the practitioners themselves, with the kinds of deeper insight which will inform and enhance their professional practice.

The sequence, then, has been from the empirical via the narrative to the developmental. And, by such a sequence, we have endeavoured to provide a firm research base for both the making of sound policy and the promotion of the professional development of practitioners.

Experience tells us that we have made some progress in this direction, that we have been able to offer research findings which practitioners are seeing certainly as challenging, but also as illuminative and helpful to their professional concerns, and, further, that we are beginning through the research to find ways of supporting practitioners in their efforts towards a continuing form of professional development.

If this is so, then our research methodologies in themselves deserve analysis and close consideration. And this we are seeking to give it in parallel with the conduct of the research itself. The links between research and development have thus provided an important secondary focus for our work.

Readers will be able to judge for themselves from the account which follows not only the value of the work of this project in relation to early years provsion, but perhaps also the merits of this qualitative and developmental approach to educational research.

1

The quality of provision in the early years: gathering the data

As we indicated in our Introduction, the purpose of this research is not merely to discover what is happening in the field of early childhood education, but, more importantly, to do so in order to secure a base from which a contribution might be made to the process of improving its quality.

The major activity during Phase One, the first year of the project, therefore, was an extensive survey of existing provision for early years (0–8) education in England and Wales. For we needed a clearer picture of current provision in all its complexities before we could either evaluate its effectiveness or enter upon Phase Two which is concerned with raising the quality of existing provision.

This survey has included all forms of provision for children from 0 to 8 in group settings, whether these are state maintained, independent or voluntary. And, while we appreciated the important differences in the legal requirements for provision for children from 0 to 5 and those from (rising) 5 to 8, and have taken full note of them in this research, the decision to include all forms of provision for children from 0 to 8 was taken both to conform to what is the internationally recognized period of early learning and to gain as full a picture as possible of all forms of group provision, including infant schools and departments.

The survey had two major dimensions. First, it sought to obtain information concerning the *nature* of provision. In particular, it explored what seem to be major determinants of quality – the settings in which the provision is made, for example, the levels of resourcing and the qualifications of all kinds of practitioners who are working with young children.

Second, however, since the ultimate aim of the project has from the beginning been to enhance the *quality* of provision, the survey also had a qualitative dimension. This aspect of the research was approached by seeking to elicit, both through the national survey itself and by a series of structured interviews, the views of those directly involved in education in the early years concerning what might constitute quality of provision. The hope was that some kind of consensus view might emerge which might be strong enough both to discount any possible charges of subjectivity and to provide a sound base upon which to build the developmental work of Phase Two in relation to both policies and practices in the early years.

The preliminary findings of the national survey are recorded in Chapter 2. This preliminary analysis is further extended in Chapter 3, where the findings are discussed in the context of previous and current policies and their effects on the nature and quality of provision. The qualitative dimension of the research is explored and analysed more fully in Chapter 4, which attempts a narrative analysis of all the relevant data.

In Phase Two of the project we are seeking to move, from the foundation provided by the research findings, from research to development. This is being done via an action research approach, which was piloted during Phase One. An account of this pilot study is offered in Chapter 5, where it will be seen that this pilot study in itself also offered interesting and important data.

The nature and sources of the Phase One research data

There were thus three main sources of research data during Phase One of the PiP project:

- The pilot action research studies, to which we have just referred.
- A series of structured interviews.
- A national survey of early years provision in England and Wales.

The pilot action research studies

In the course of the year, eleven pilot studies were undertaken, and these were in a range of early years schools and other group settings in both the maintained and the independent sectors. All were in the London area.

These pilot studies began by examining the claim that, if we are to develop the quality of the curriculum for young children, then we must have reflective practitioners. In each study, a member of the research team worked with a practitioner in order to test this assumption by evaluating the effect that reflection on practice had on both the quality and the development of practice and provision. In line with the action research tradition, the nature of the data which emerged from these case studies was personal to, and under the control of, each individual action researcher. However, both the case studies themselves and the evaluations of them by members of the project team offered insights which illuminated and amplified the data gleaned from the other sources.

Structured interviews

The structured interviews were conducted with the heads of those early years settings in which the action research pilot studies were being simultaneously undertaken. They were designed to explore in depth, and by a different research technique, issues of quality, and to complement the evidence derived from those questions on the questionnaire which were directed at eliciting comments on the perceived determinants of quality.

The use of interviews to gain deeper insights into the realities of particular situations and, especially, the views and values of the actors within those situations is a well established research technique. It has been claimed (Patton, 1980, p. 196) to be the best way 'to find out what is on someone else's mind'. It was precisely this kind of information we were seeking.

It is a technique, however, which has its dangers and pitfalls, since as Helen Simons has said (1977, p. 27), 'relying as it does . . . on the personal skills and judgments of the interviewer it is also open to manipulation and distortion'. At the very least, since these personal skills will vary from one interviewer to another, and since the interpersonal dynamics of every interactive situation will be unique, there are dangers that what seems to emerge as data will be valueless.

A number of techniques have been adopted in the attempt to obviate these dangers. One of those employed here was to establish guidelines for structured interviews, to lay down principles of procedure to 'protect both the interviewer and the interviewee from misuse of data' (*ibid.*, p. 27).

A second device we adopted was to tape-record every interview. A disadvantage here is the inhibiting effect this may have on the person being interviewed. This we found, however, was not as great as the inhibition which almost always accompanies the taking of extensive notes by the interviewer. And it is further offset by the acquisition of an accurate record of data – an acquisition which of course depends crucially on the accuracy and quality of the subsequent transcript.

Lastly, every effort was made to avoid allowing those interviewed to slip into a passive role. In so far as was possible, each interview was conducted as a 'conversation between fellow professionals', and the guidelines, although there to ensure some kind of objectivity through standardization, were not permitted to impose rigidity or to depersonalize the activity.

These interviews, then, which are audio-taped, were all conducted in accordance with agreed standard guidelines (see Appendix A). And, although the level of funding only allowed us to conduct eleven such interviews at Phase One, this pilot exercise has enabled us to compare modes of analysis to determine which are the most appropriate and productive for this form of qualitative exploration, and to extend this research activity at Phase Two.

The national survey

The concern of Chapter 2 of this report is to set out the major findings from the statistical survey. These findings will then be amplified in the later chapters, with some elaboration and elucidation derived from the interviews and the pilot action research case studies. Before we embark on detailing these findings, however, it is important to say something about the ways in which the survey was planned and the data collected.

The design of the survey

The survey was conducted through a questionnaire (see Appendix B). Our targeted respondents were from a cross-section of institutions/ groups and ranged from headteachers in schools to leaders of playgroups. We needed a questionnaire, therefore, which, while being appropriately wide ranging, would not create any major difficulties for the respondents. To ensure this, it was decided to pilot test the questionnaire and invite evaluation of it by practitioners before the main survey was undertaken.

The main aims of the questionnaire were to:

- elicit information on the nature and qualifications of practitioners working with children under 8;
- identify key factors or criteria that support the development of an appropriate curriculum for young children;
- identify key factors or criteria that constrain the development of an appropriate curriculum for young children;
- identify key factors that are influential in the professional development of practitioners working with young children;
- obtain the views of practitioners concerning what constitutes a quality curriculum for young children;
- obtain practitioners' suggestions for improvements in the current educational provision for under-8s; and

- obtain practitioners' suggestions for improvements in professional training and development for practitioners who work with young children.

The final version of the questionnaire was designed in three parts:
- *Part I:* information related to the institution.
- *Part II:* number and qualifications of staff.
- *Part III:* The quality of early learning.

The fifteen questions posed in Parts I and II were designed to elicit factual information. The five questions in Part III, however, sought the views of the heads of institutions on the quality of early learning and the factors which they felt supported or constrained that quality.

The survey aimed to give both a representative picture of national provision and a more detailed picture of provision in one selected region of the country. The subjects of the main survey, therefore, were selected from two main groups:

- All local authorities in the Greater London area.
- Selected counties and cities in England and Wales which would give a representative picture of national provision.

The geographical locations selected are shown in Table 1.1.

Information was then gathered for all types of provision in the selected areas under the following categories:

State-maintained provision
- nursery schools
- infant and first schools
- primary schools
- special schools and units
- local authority day nurseries

Non-maintained provision
- independent preparatory schools
- independent nursery schools
- private and workplace nurseries
- playgroups

Survey questionnaires were sent to a representative sample of each category of provision.

A detailed discussion of the basis on which these samples were chosen and a justification of the methodology used may be found in the Phase One report of the first year's work of the project (Blenkin *et al.*, 1995). And a synopsis of this discussion is included at Appendix C. Two points are worth noting here, however.

Table 1.1 Geographical locations selected for the questionnaire survey

London boroughs	*Selected counties and cities in*
Barking & Dagenham	*England and Wales*
Barnet	Berkshire
Bexley	Buckinghamshire
Brent	Cambridgeshire
Bromley	Devon
Camden	Gwynedd
City of London	Hampshire
Croydon	Humberside
Ealing	Isle of Man
Enfield	Isle of Wight
Greenwich	Kent
Hackney	Kirklees
Hammersmith & Fulham	Liverpool
Harringey	Manchester
Harrow	Norfolk
Havering	North Tyneside
Hillingdon	North Yorkshire
Hounslow	Nottinghamshire
Islington	South Glamorgan
Kensington & Chelsea	Wolverhampton
Kingston upon Thames	
Lambeth	
Lewisham	
Merton	
Newham	
Redbridge	
Richmond	
Southwark	
Sutton	
Tower Hamlets	
Waltham Forest	
Wandsworth	
Westminster	

First, the total number of nursery schools and day nurseries in both the maintained and the independent sectors was so small that *all* these nurseries in the selected regions were surveyed rather than a sample. This was the first intimation of the paucity of provision of this kind and level. It also came as something of a surprise in relation to all the political statements of expansion in this area which have emerged regularly for the last three decades.

Second, considerable difficulties were encountered in identifying local authority day nurseries. For it was found that twelve different names are used to denote these in the 52 LEAs which were selected

Table 1.2 Different names used to represent local authority day nurseries

Day nursery
Children's centre
Young children's centre
Family centre
Under-5s centre
Under-8s centre
Day centre
Nursery centre
Under-5s resource centre
Under-5s education centre (UFEC)
Early years centre
Childcare centre

(Table 1.2). This proliferation of names was confusing to the experienced professionals of the research team. It must, therefore, be even more confusing to parents seeking appropriate provision for their children. Similar confusion was found to exist also in the designation of playgroup settings, where a significant number were described as private nurseries, probably for reasons of commerce or status. Indeed, this interpretation seems to be confirmed by the fact that, since we conducted our survey, all playgroups have been formally renamed as preschools.

Ultimately, however, a total random sample of 2,420 educational and non-educational establishments, representing all forms of under-8s provision, was chosen for the main survey, and a questionnaire was sent to each of these. As predicted, just under a quarter of these (548) had been returned by the designated date. Details are given in Table 1.3. Since this constituted a valid sample, the analysis of the data could then be undertaken. This analysis is detailed in the chapters which follow.

Table 1.3 Total number of questionnaires returned

Type of provision	Total returned from London	Total returned from the counties	Total returned	Percentage of total sent
Nursery schools	43	47	90	49
Infant/first schools	26	47	73	45
Primary schools	42	46	88	23
Special schools	24	26	60	21
Local authority day nurseries	17	4	21	12
Independent preparatory schools	27	34	61	20
Independent nursery schools	10	14	24	37
Private/workplace nurseries	25	11	36	12
Playgroups	59	36	95	22
Sum of all provisions	273	275	548	23

Note: Total number of questionnaires sent = 2,420.

2

The realities of working with young children in group settings: some first impressions from the survey

---

This chapter will set out the findings which emerged from our preliminary analysis of the survey data. We were concerned, at this early stage of the analysis, to scrutinize the findings from those sections of the survey data which were designed to explore the quantitative issues we have identified as providing the basis from which our qualitative survey could be mounted. They represent what might be seen as matters of fact, those details of the conditions under which early childhood provision is currently being made in England and Wales.

It is beyond the scope of this book to set these out in great detail. They are available in the full report of Phase One of the research (Blenkin *et al.*, 1995), and we will provide precise references to this for the benefit of readers who wish to pursue any of the aspects of the survey in greater detail. Our intentions here are to highlight significant aspects of these findings and, in doing so, to identify the important themes which began to emerge from the analysis of the data at this early stage.

The data which have emerged from the quantitative survey fall into two main categories. The first of these relates to the practitioners. This of course is the prime focus of the research as a whole.

The second provides background information relating to the children (0–8) who are to be found in these group settings – their gender, their first language, their mode of attendance (whether full or part time) and the staff:child ratios. It also includes findings concerning the the group settings themselves, the institutions in which the children are to be found – their geographical location and environment, their financial, legal and administrative status, and the kinds of accommodation they enjoy, whether shared, for example, or available for sole use.

Most of this latter information is of course already available from other sources, such as the records held by the Department for

Education. In the context of this project, it was sought in order to provide a background for our survey. Our first analysis of the data, therefore, set out to provide a picture of the nature of group provision and some factual information about those children who attend. We chose to analyse this section of the data first because our intention was to set the main analysis of data relating to early years practitioners and the quality of their professional practice against important background information concerning the context in which they worked. This would, we hoped, provide us with evidence on which we could develop realistic strategies to support professional development.

Having set the background, we then turned our attention to the main focus – the practitioners. Here our concern was to learn more about their initial training and qualifications, and their subsequent in-service experience. We were seeking also to obtain information about the roles they fulfil in relation to the care and education of the children. And, finally, we wanted to elicit their views on what they see as constituting quality in the early years curriculum, as a basis for the qualitative dimension of the research.

We begin the report of our first impressions from the survey, however, with the preliminary findings about the context of early years provision, starting with a summary of those findings related to the children.

Preliminary findings about the context of early years provision

Only three of the survey's questions were directly concerned with the children, and these sought to elicit information about their attendance patterns, the proportion of boys and girls and the number of children with English as a second language. This information was categorized under each year group from birth to 8, and this categorization gave us an opportunity to evaluate differential patterns, especially in those institutions providing for children of non-statutory age (0–5).

Our findings show, first, that the proportion of boys and girls attending early years group provision is almost equal (boys 51.7%; girls 48.3%). This overall even proportion is a feature of most of the different types of provision, with the balance slightly in favour of boys. Girls are in a slight majority, however, in playgroups and in mixed independent preparatory schools, although again not in significant numbers. The findings show that, by and large, attendance proportions of boys and girls match those of the whole population of under-8s in England and Wales, where boys are in a slight majority.

There is, however, one significant exception. The proportion of boys

Table 2.1 Proportion of full-time and part-time children in under-8s institutions (%)

	Full time	Part time
Nursery schools (*n=87*)	20.9	79. 1
Infant/first schools (*n=71*)	83.4	16.6
Primary schools (*n=83*)	92.3	7.7
Special schools (*n=52*)	83.4	16.6
Local authority day nurseries (*n=21*)	57.8	42.2
Independent prep schools (*n=58*)	84.9	15.1
Independent nursery schools (*n=24*)	46.3	53.7
Private/workplace nurseries (*n=34*)	45.1	54.9
Playgroups (*n=91*)	18.5	81.5
All provisions (*n=521*)	58.0	42.0
State-maintained provisions (*n=314*)	66.7	33.3
Non-maintained provisions (*n=207*)	44.7	55.3
London (all provisions) (*n=260*)	56.1	43.9

attending special schools, according to our survey, is significantly larger than that of girls (boys 63%; girls 37%). The reasons for this imbalance are open to speculation and may relate to medical, social or other factors. Certainly further research into the reasons would be of interest, although it is beyond the scope of the PiP project.

Other than this, the evidence from our survey shows that the over-whelming pattern of attendance by boys and girls broadly matches the proportions in the population as a whole and very little of new significance emerges from the factual evidence on gender (Blenkin *et al.*, 1995, p. 153).

Our figures on attendance, part time and full time, however, give a more uneven picture (Table 2.1). They show that, although just over half (58%) of the children who are attending are full-timers, this figure changes dramatically when attendance in groups providing only for children of non-statutory age are considered. Only 21% of children in state nursery schools and 45% of children in private and workplace nurseries, for example, attend full time, and there is no significant difference in the figures for the London area when compared with those for the country as a whole (*op. cit.*, p. 151).

Further than this, our findings on attendance also show that, while two-thirds (66.7%) of children in the state-maintained sector are full-timers, over half (55.3%) of those in the voluntary and independent sectors are part time only. It is thus clear that, when attendance figures for schools providing for children of statutory school age are removed, the majority of provision for under-5s is being made on a part-time basis and largely in the non-maintained sectors. Some of the reasons for these differential patterns are explored in the next chapter. It is worth noting here, however, that universal state nursery provision for those parents who want it for their children is still a distant goal and one which is also a long way from being attainable in the non-maintained sector for those parents who can afford to pay for it.

It is also worth noting here that a further implication of this high proportion of part-time attendance is its implications for staff:pupil ratios. For, in relation to part-time attendance, the figures (which we shall see later) for staffing ratios conceal the fact that the actual number of pupils for which any one practitioner is responsible is, for example, where provision is on a half-time basis, twice as high as the level indicated by the bare ratios. And this further entails up to twice as many families with which the practitioner must collaborate.

Our findings on the number of children with English as a second language highlight equally interesting issues in relation to policy, provision and need. Over one-tenth (11.3%) of all the children attending early years provision in group settings do not have English as their mother tongue, and this proportion becomes significantly higher in the London area (16.9%). The findings also show clearly that by far a majority of these bilingual young children are attending in the state-maintained sector. For example, the proportion in all types of main-atined provision is almost double that in the non-maintained sector (13.7% compared to 7.3%), and this differential is even greater in nursery schools, where the proportion in state nurseries is over three times that in the independent sector (*op cit.*, p. 153).

Not surprisingly, our figures show a much higher number of bi-lingual children in the London area compared to the country as a whole. Indeed, it is highly likely that this differential proportion would be repeated in other conurbations if similar surveys were made. For it is in the inner-city areas, and particularly in London, that new immi-grants are most likely to settle. It is also interesting to note that a much higher proportion attend provision in the maintained sector than in other sectors, although the reasons for this are not clear cut. The ex-planation may be, for example, economic circumstances. Alternatively, the disproportion may be a result of decisions made by local education authorities and other providers in the maintained sector to direct re-sources to support young children who are at the beginning stages of learning English during this critical period of early childhood.

Overall, our data on the children and their patterns of attendance offer one fascinating perspective on the working conditions in the different types of early years settings, and we will return to a fuller discussion of this in Chapter 3. We turn now, however, to a summary of the general findings relating to the institutions themselves, including such important factors as their financial status and the accommodation that is available to them.

Our survey revealed that over half (52.5%) of all institutions are funded by local authorities, including all the maintained nursery schools and local authority day nurseries, nearly all infant schools (93.2%) and special schools (96.7%), and the great majority of primary schools with nursery classes (80.7%). This contrasts sharply with playgroups – or preschools, as groups that are members of the Preschool Learning Alliance are now known – where only two in one hundred (2.1%) are funded by local authorities. As pointed out by the Audit Commission (1996), this has enforced upon playgroups a low level of funding which has resulted in their not being able to afford either the staff pay or the funded training opportunities which would enable them to build on the commitment and enthusiasm of so many of their workers.

Just over a third of institutions – a surpisingly high proportion – are funded independently (34.4%). These include all the preparatory schools and independent nursery schools, three-fifths (61.8%) of private and workplace nurseries, almost half (46.3%) of playgroups or preschools, and a small proportion of special schools (1.7%).

The rest are financed in various ways – voluntarily (6.3%), through grant-maintained status (0.7%), by employers (3.6%) or from other sources (2.5%) (*op. cit.*, p. 147).

In respect of funding, therefore, our findings reveal an immensely complex picture. And this is especially the case in the provision made for the non-statutory age-groups and within the independent and voluntary sectors. This complexity would seem to suggest that the establishment of provision for the under-5s is not the only problem. The arrangements for the funding of that provision also need to be simplified somewhat.

Clearly, the financial status of the institutions is also likely to influence the resources available, in particular the accommodation and staffing levels. The survey sought evidence of such links, first through information about accommodation. Two questions addressed the issue of accommodation – one concerning whether or not this was shared, and the other about safe and easy access to outdoor as well as indoor environments. Both sets of responses gave us a good indication of the quality of the working environments in the different sectors.

The cases of shared accommodation are distributed fairly evenly across all sectors, with one significant exception. Playgroups (now preschools) share their accommodation to a far greater extent than other kinds of provision (Table 2.2). Over a fifth of all institutions shared their accommodation, but within this almost three-quarters of

Table 2.2   Sharing of accommodation in under-8s institutions (%)

	Percent sharing accommodation
Nursery schools (*n*=90)	5.6
Infant/first schools (*n*=73)	23.3
Primary schools (*n*=88)	11.4
Special schools (*n*=59)	18.6
Local authority day nurseries (*n*=21)	19.0
Independent prep schools (*n*=61) (mixed school only)	9.8
Independent nursery schools (*n*=24)	20.8
Private/workplace nurseries (*n*=36)	13.9
Playgroups (*n*=94)	74.5
All provisions (*n*=546)	21.9
State-maintained provisions (*n*=331)	15.6
Non-maintained provisions (*n*=215)	29.8
London (all provisions) (*n*=271)	25.1
London (state-maintained) (*n*=151)	16.5
London (non-maintained) (*n*=120)	35.8
Counties (all provisions) (*n*=275)	20.1
Counties (state-maintained) (*n*=180)	16.2
Counties (non-maintained) (*n*=95)	25.0

playgroups (74.5%) shared theirs. Even the private and workplace nurseries were largely (13.9%) unable to call their accommodation their own, with all that this implies in terms of being able to make permanent and semi-permanent dispositions of furniture and equipment and being able to leave children's work for them to continue the next day.

It should be said, however, that there are clearly different degrees of sharing, and it would be helpful to know more about what particular aspects were most difficult for staff to deal with. Sharing a playground with the primary school could be a considerable problem for infant teachers, for instance. It may be that light will be shed on this aspect by the work of the action researchers in Phase Two, many of whom are very interested in outdoor play and have chosen this theme as their research focus.

The proportion of institutions in the non-maintained sector who share their accommodation is almost double that in the state-maintained sector (29.8% versus 15.6%). Just one in five (20.1%) institutions in the counties share their accommodation compared with one in four (25.1%) in London (*op. cit.*, p. 148). This may be an indication of differences in the cost of establishing such provision in different regions of the country.

Other differentials between the several sectors of provision become evident when the data on the children's access to outdoor play spaces are examined. For, although outdoor spaces are available in nearly all types of eary years setting (92.7%), and continuous access to this outdoor space is possible in over two-thirds of institutions (70.2%), the figures on both availability and use within individual types – in other words, both their access to the out-of-doors and the ways in which the staff make use of this facility – reveal discrepancies between high-level use of this provision. And this discrepancy shows not only between institutions in the different sectors but also between those catering for different age-groups.

For example, most schools within the maintained and independent sectors have 100% access to an outdoor play space. This facility is not universally available, however, to playgroups (preschools) in the voluntary sector, although access is available to the majority of such groups (84.2%). A dramatically different picture emerges, however, from the evidence on the use of the outdoor play space. Respondents were asked whether, if it was available the outdoor play space was used continuously, occasionally or rarely. Their answers show that continuous access is available for the majority of children in maintained nursery schools (91.1%), but this level of access drops dramatically both for children of statutory school age (53.4%, for example, in state infant schools) and for those in playgroups (42.1%) (*op. cit.*, p. 150). This low level of use of outdoor facilities clearly has important implications for concerns of health and fitness. It is also of particular significance if one takes account of the fact that many parents look to institutions to provide their children with opportunities for outdoor play in secure environments, since increasingly such opportunities cannot be assured within the context of the wider community.

An equally interesting picture emerges from what the survey reveals about staff:child ratios. The figures, which include full-time and part-time staff, show that the average number of children per member of staff across all types of provision is nine (Table 2.3). Not surprisingly, special schools have the most favourable ratio (1:2). The ratio is slightly more favourable in the non-maintained as opposed to the maintained sector (1:7 *versus* 1:11). Further than this, independent preparatory schools maintain the average (1:9) ratio for their under-8s, whereas the least favourable ratios are to be found in state-maintained primary schools (*op. cit.*, p. 155).

This early analysis of the staff:child ratios, of course, is based purely on numbers of adults and children within each setting. It does not, therefore, reveal more subtle details, such as the training and status of staff and the effect of this on provision. Nor does it indicate whether

Table 2.3   Staff:child ratio for under-8s institutions

	Staff:child ratio
Nursery schools (*n=87*)	1:13
Infant/first schools (*n=68*)	1:12
Primary schools (*n=80*)	1:15
Special schools (*n=52*)	1:2
Local authority day nurseries (*n=19*)	1:4
Independent prep schools (*n=54*) (mixed school only)	1:9
Independent nursery schools (*n=24*)	1:8
Private/workplace nurseries (*n=33*)	1:5
Playgroups (*n=87*)	1:7
All provisions (*n=504*)	1:9
State-maintained provisions (*n=306*)	1:11
Non-maintained provisions (*n=198*)	1:7
London (all provisions) (*n=253*)	1:9

Note: Number of staff includes both full time and part time.

staffing levels are a consequence of the provider's choices on such issues as cost or are the result of statutory requirements for childcare and education. These subtleties will be considered later.

Two aspects, however, must be highlighted in the context of this discussion. First, provision for very young infants, especially for those under 3 years of age, is labour intensive, and this is reflected in our findings. For example, in local authority day nurseries and private/workplace nurseries, where most of the very young children in group care are being looked after, the ratios are favourable (1:4 and 1:5, respectively).

Second, the current levels of staff:child ratios in state nursery, infant and primary schools are the least favourable of all the categories (1:13, 1:12 and 1:15, respectively). It is important to highlight this evidence and its implications for class sizes in the maintained sector. For such ratios must be a constraint on the quality of provision, in spite of greater advantages in terms of accommodation and the qualifications of staff (*ibid.*, p. 155).

Furthermore, as we saw earlier, this is also compounded by the fact that, in a high proportion of state-maintained nursery schools and classes, where the pattern of attendance is half time, the actual number of children for which any one full-time practitioner will be responsible, and the number of families with which he or she must collaborate, will be twice as many as suggested by the bare staff:pupil ratio.

This, then, is the background which the early analysis of our data provided. It is against this background that we now consider our

Table 2.4   Qualifications held by heads of institutions (%)

BA(Ed)/BEd/BAdd	19.2
BA	14.9
BSc	3.3
NNEB/City & Guilds	18.3
SRN	1.0
PGCE	9.0
NVQs	0.8
BTech	0.6
MA/MEd/MAdd	11.1
Cert. Ed. (2 years)	10.4
Cert. Ed. (3 years)	31.7
Montessori Certificate	5.2
PPA short courses	13.0
PPA Diploma in Playgroup Practice	10.5
PPA Tutor & Fieldwork Course	1.2
PPA Further Course	3.7
MPhiL/PhD	1.4
None	0.4
Others	31.8
More than one qualification	57.6

Note: n=536.

preliminary findings concerning the practitioners themselves.

Preliminary findings about the practitioners

The survey has produced a clear picture of the kinds of training undertaken by those practitioners who work with young children and of the qualifications which they hold (Blenkin *et al.*, 1995, pp. 15–96). Some salient points, however, need to be highlighted here.

If we consider first the heads of the group settings, an interesting picture emerges (Table 2.4). A significant feature is that this is an ageing group; and this is particularly true of those who are headteachers. For example, just over two-fifths (42.1%) of the heads of institutions were qualified through a Certificate of Education, a form of qualification which disappeared in the early 1980s when teaching became an all-graduate profession. Further, of this group, a quarter (24.7%) qualified before 1960 with a two-year certificate. In all, therefore, fewer than two-fifths (37.4%) have first degrees. Those who do usually have degrees in education (BA(Ed), BEd, BAdd).

A significant number of heads of institutions, however, have no teaching background. One third (28.4%) have playgroup qualifications accredited by the PreSchool Playgroup Association (PPA) (now known

Table 2.5   Qualifications held by under-8s practitioners (%)

BA(Ed)/BEd/BAdd	13.8
BA	4.0
BSc	1.5
NNEB/City & Guilds	20.9
SRN	0.9
PGCE	3.3
NVQs	0.5
MA/MEd/MAdd	0.8
MPhill/PhD	0.1
BTech	0.8
Cert. Ed. (2 years)	2.2
Cert. Ed. (3 years)	15.8
Montessori Certificate	2.4
PPA Diploma in Playgroup Practice	7.9
PPA Tutor & Fieldwork Course	0.5
PPA short courses	6.6
PPA further course	1.5
None	10.4
Others	6.1
More than one qualification	7.0

Note: n=530.

as the Pre-School Learning Alliance – PLA), and just under one-fifth (18.3%) were qualified by way of NNEB/City & Guilds courses.

More than half these heads hold more than one qualification. Most of these additional qualifications are clearly related to career moves into specialist professional areas – diplomas in special needs, for example, certificates in special education and so on. A little more than one-tenth (12.5%) have higher degree qualifications, of which the vast majority (88.8%) are taught masters' degrees rather than research degrees.

The qualifications of the practitioners working directly with children under 8, as opposed to those who are heads of institutions, are of a significantly lower level (Table 2.5). For example, only 19.3% of all practitioners have a first degree; and of these, as with the heads' group, most (71.5%) hold a first degree in education. The largest group is that of those who qualified by way of NNEB/City & Guilds courses. A very low proportion (0.9%) have a higher degree. And more than 10% of practitioners hold no qualifications at all.

These figures reveal, therefore, that, despite the fact that entry to the teaching sector of early years provision currently depends upon graduate status, most practitioners in post, including teacher practitioners, do not have this. Thus the profession of early years practitioners as a whole is far from being a graduate profession.

Furthermore, the survey revealed that, even among those

Table 2.6   Age ranges for which qualified teachers working with under-8s were initially trained (%)

Age range	
3–5	8.2
3–8	16.8
5–7	9.5
3–11	9.3
5–11	29.7
7–11	10.2
11–16	9.7
Others	6.6

Note: n=360.

practitioners holding qualifications which carry qualified teacher status, a minority had been specifically trained to work with early years children. Many of the qualifications listed in the survey questionnaire, such as the NNEB certificate and the PPA diplomas, relate directly to work undertaken with young children. This is not true, however, of teaching qualifications.

The survey asked a quite specific question about the age phases for which those qualified teachers working with the under-8s had been trained. The response to this question is highly informative (Table 2.6).

For only a quarter (25%) of the qualified teachers working in this sector had been initially trained for the 3–8 age phase; and, of these, only one-third (32.8%) were initially trained for the 3–5 age phase. A further 9.3% had had a form of initial training which included some work with under-5s. The majority (65.7%), however, had received no initial training specific to work with preschool children. Further, more than a quarter (26.5%) had received no initial training specific to work with under-8s.

These findings about the initial qualifications of practitioners working with young children, especially those working as qualified teachers, revealed a level of specialization which, in most cases, was either low or non-existent. And this rendered questions concerning retraining and further study particularly important, so that the section of the questionnaire which set out to explore this aspect of practitioners' qualifications gained a special significance.

The overwhelming evidence here, however, is that, once trained and qualified, practitioners are unlikely to pursue further qualifications or training of an award-bearing kind (Blenkin and Yue, 1994). Taken together with the findings concerning initial training, this offers a highly disturbing picture. For it reveals that a significant number of those working professionally with, and responsible for the education of,

Table 2.7 Factors considered by heads of institutions to be most significant in supporting the development of an appropriate curriculum for young children (%)

Supporting factors	
Qualifications of staff	25.6
Range of experience of staff	27.8
Length of experience of staff	7.2
Qualities of staff	74.2
Provision for staff development and INSET	25.3
Evaluating provision	11.1
Keeping records of children's learning	22.5
Assessment of children	24.7
Effective partnership with parents	72.1
High ratio of staff to children	43.4
Provision of an effective environment for learning	63.2
An adequate physical enviromnent for learning	13.6
A supportive social environment	13.4
High-quality resources for early learning	32.8
Adequate number of resources for early learning	25.2
Management structure of the institution/group	19.1

Note: n=544.

children under 8 have had no training, either initial or in-service, which is related specifically to the needs of young children and their families.

Furthermore, a similar pattern of career development seems to occur, albeit at different levels, across the full range of practitioners who are working with young children. And a significant feature of this pattern is that these practitioners appear to engage in further training only if it is a requirement of the post, and not either for its own sake or in the pursuit of professional development.

The data on patterns of training and levels of qualifications of early years practitioners provide important insights into how professional training might be developed from realistic starting-points. It was important for us also to establish a clearer picture of early years practitioners' views of what a quality curriculum is and the factors which support or constrain it. What follows are the views of the heads of the institutions on these issues.

The heads' views of a quality curriculum for the early years

Section Three of the questionnaire (see Appendix B) asked practitioners a number of questions in order to elicit their views concerning quality in early learning. First, the heads were offered a list of sixteen factors and asked to indicate which they felt offered the greatest support for the development of an appropriate curriculum for young children (Table 2.7).

The factors which were cited as most significant by a high proportion of respondents were 'The qualities of staff' (74.2%), 'Effective partnership with parents' (72.1%) and 'The provision of an effective environment for learning', (63.2%). Conversely, factors which were considered not so significant were 'Length of experience of staff' (7.2%), 'Evaluating provision' (11.1%), 'An adequate physical environment for learning (13.6%)' and 'A supportive social environment' (13.4%). The last of these we found somewhat surprising in the light of recent research which has shown the importance of the social environment in early learning (Wells, 1987).

'A high ratio of staff to children' was also identified as of great significance by heads of private and workplace nurseries (64.7%), heads of independent nursery schools (62.5%) and playgroup leaders (57.4%) (Blenkin *et al.*, 1995, pp. 97–114).

The effectiveness of staff within the workplace – whether school, nursery or playgroup – was emphasized by heads from every kind of provision as the most important factor in the provision of an appropriate curriculum for young children. This was expressed, as we have just seen, through their ranking of 'The qualities of staff', which was the most open of the list of factors offered. The more obvious factors related to staff training, on the other hand, 'Qualifications of staff' and 'Provision for staff development and INSET', which might have been seen as assisting members of staff to acquire the necessary qualities, were ranked very low by all heads except those in independent preparatory schools. This would seem to indicate a mistrust by practitioners of what they may regard as academic intellectualism. And it is less than encouraging when one is working to improve the quality of the early years curriculum through attempting to enhance the reflective powers of practitioners.

Also of interest is the fact that, when the heads were next asked to identify from a further list those factors which they regard as constraining the development of a quality curriculum (Table 2.8), most of them emphasized practical factors rather than those concerned with values. For example, 'Insufficient budget for resources' (60.3%) and 'Poor management of the institution' (55.8%) were regarded as very significant constraining factors.

Further, a majority of heads (62.9%) in all types of provision, except state-maintained nursery schools, cited 'Inadequate levels of staffing' as the most constraining factor. Most of the nursery headteachers (73.3%), however, emphasized 'Staff not trained for early years specialism' (Table 2.9). This was one of the few occasions when the responses linked training to quality of provision.

We noted earlier the low level of use of outdoor facilities. It is not

Table 2.8 Factors considered by heads of institutions to be most significant in constraining the development of an appropriate curriculum for young children (%)

Constraining factors	
Staff not trained for early years specialism	53.1
Inexperienced staff	41.7
Inadequate levels of staffing	62.9
Lack of opportunities for staff training and INSET	32.3
Poor monitoring of provision	26.6
Inappropriate procedures for assessing children	36.7
Inadequate provision for parental involvement	46.2
Restricted space for learning	26.1
Inappropriate accommodation	38.9
Limited opportunities for learning out of doors	12.5
Insufficient budget for resources	60.3
Poor management of the institution	55.8

Note: n=543.

Table 2.9 Factors considered by heads of nursery schools to be most significant in constraining the development of an appropriate curriculum for young children (%)

Constraining factors	
Staff not trained for early years specialism	73.3
Inexperienced staff	11.1
Inadequate levels of staffing	65.6
Lack of opportunities for staff training and INSET	35.6
Poor monitoring of provision	36.7
Inappropriate procedures for assessing children	36.7
Inadequate provision for parental involvement	42.2
Restricted space for learning	21.1
Inappropriate accommodation	42.2
Limited opportunities for learning out of doors	30.0
Insufficient budget for resources	36.7
Poor management of the institution	66.7

Note: n=90.

surprising, therefore, to find that only a relatively small proportion (12.5%) identified 'Limited opportunities for learning out of doors' as a significant constraint. This may indicate a traditional, 'academic' concept of curriculum as concerned mainly with quiet, indoor learning. As we commented above, however, it is of concern to find that outdoor activities are not regarded by practitioners as important at a time when for considerations of safety parents are increasingly reluctant to allow young children out of doors, and, indeed, when many of them send their children to school or playgroup in order deliberately to ensure that they have opportunities for outdoor play (Blenkin et. al., 1995, pp. 115–30).

Table 2.10 Factors considered to be influential in the professional development of practitioners by the heads of institutions

Influential factors	Ranking point
Knowledge of child development	1.82
Ability to assess individual child	3.34
Organizational skills	3.42
Partnership with parents	4.24
Openness to change	4.60
Meticulous planning	5.46
Regular staff meetings	5.78
Understanding of educational issues	5.89
Knowledge of school subjects	6.73
Feedback from staff appraisal	7.14
School-based in-service training	7.15
Local authority based in-service training	8.12
Familiarity with recent research	8.63
Higher education-based in-service training	9.61
Access to professional journals	9.81

Notes: n=534; Ranking point 1=the most influential factor.

In pursuance of our underlying concern with professional development, the third question which heads were asked to address in this section of the questionnaire invited them to identify factors which they considered influential in the professional development of practitioners working with under-8s.

The responses to this question produced one of the most noteworthy findings of the questionnaire survey. For the majority of heads, in every form of group setting – voluntary, independent and state-maintained – ranked 'Knowledge of child development' as the single most important factor in the professional development of practitioners (Table 2.10). On the other hand, 'Knowledge of school subjects' was ranked relatively low even by those respondents who were heads of schools for children of statutory age – state-maintained primary and infant schools and preparatory schools in the private sector (*op. cit.*, pp. 131–46).

These responses offer almost a consensus view across all the different types of group provision. And this view is of considerable significance in the light of current policies for the initial training of early years teachers. For the effect of government's current policy has been to discontinue specialist early years training, for example by excluding the study of child development from primary training courses and replacing it with National Curriculum subject studies. That policy thus ignores what has emerged as the views of experienced practitioners of all kinds on what constitutes appropriate professional knowledge for those working with young children.

In addition to 'Knowledge of child development', respondents ranked 'Ability to assess individual children', 'Organizational skills' and 'Partnership with parents' as of high significance in the professional development of early years practitioners. Conversely, in-service training of all kinds was again considered to be of less significance.

In general, what has emerged from this section of our survey is a remarkable consensus of view, among heads from all kinds of setting, about quality in the early years curriculum. Furthermore, that consensus is characterized by profiles which are again remarkably similar. There is, for example, a conviction that what constitutes quality in the early years curriculum is a focus on the child and the person. And this in turn determines what is regarded as constituting relevant professional knowledge. Thus a knowledge of child development and an ability to work closely in partnership with parents are regarded as indispensable to effective practice, whereas subject knowledge is seen as less crucial.

There is also a negative attitude to be found in these profiles. For they reveal an indifference towards training and professional development, which may perhaps be at odds with the positive consensus view of essential professional qualities. This indifference may derive from an anti-intellectualism and a consequent distrust of higher-level training or it may reflect a diffidence on the part of the practitioners concerning their own abilities to succeed at that level. Whatever the explanation, this is a factor which must be addressed if we are right to see professional development as the only effective route to improving quality of provision.

These, then, are the first impressions concerning the realities of working with young children which have emerged from the preliminary analysis of the quantitative data from our research. Our next task was to identify patterns within the data, seeking differentials which seemed to be of interest to practitioners and policy-makers alike, and to seek links with historical and administrative developments in the field of early childhood education.

Chapter 3, therefore, attempts to identify such patterns and to explore the historical and administrative context in which provision for young children has been developed. In doing so, it will offer a deeper analysis of our findings and seek to explain them by reference to the impact of social and political policies on the working lives of practitioners.

3

Practitioners and early years provision: patterns from the data

Chapter 2 has drawn the outline of what the survey has shown, and has demonstrated some important facets of practitioners' views. In particular, it has shown that their definitions of a quality curriculum and the factors supporting and constraining it reveal a marked consensus in certain important areas, as do their views on what factors are influential in the professional development of practitioners. Yet at the same time there are very wide differences of experience and perspective which are reflected in the findings. And patterns emerged as we scrutinized those findings in greater depth.

It is the role of this chapter to explore these findings in greater detail and, through reflecting on them as they apply to particular groups of practitioners, to try to get a sense of the major concerns and issues of their working lives, and how these affect the provision of a quality curriculum in the early years. The different qualifications, working circumstances and status of practitioners influence their provision for children's learning as can be seen in the different themes and emphases that emerge from the data. We also discover from these responses the principles practitioners bring to their thinking about the curriculum, and where they have reached in their reflections. These principles are the practitioners' criteria of quality and, together with their ideas about how the curriculum can be provided, they are the starting-point in the search for improvements in the quality of provision for young children's learning. It is on this foundation that achievable strategies for development must be built.

In this chapter we aim, therefore, to establish more clearly a picture of the people who are providing care and education in group settings in the early years, the conditions in which they work, their qualifications and the impact of their circumstances on the way they think about their task. We shall seek to do this by filling in some of the background to both the survey data and the structured interviews which supplied the in-depth perspectives that illuminate the statistical data for us. The personal aspects of practitioners' thinking emerge particularly clearly in the narratives given in response to Questions 19 and 20 of the questionnaire, and these will be analysed in Chapter 4. This chapter will provide a framework for the personal interpretations by looking at the background to these responses and some of the particular characteristics they evince about broad issues to do with early childhood education in general and the curriculum in particular.

In this way we hope to reveal something of the diverse circumstances and concerns within which our respondents ground their thinking and doing, and what their responses can tell us about the needs of practitioners as they seek to develop and improve their practice.

We will concentrate in particular on the similarities and differences between the different sectors of maintained education, maintained care, voluntary and independent, and the patterns of training, funding and organization which characterize each sector. In addition, where relevant, we will highlight any significant similarities and differences between London and the counties that the evidence offers.

These features inter-relate within the field of early childhood care and education and are simultaneously affected by policy and legislation at central and local government levels. Because of the distinctive structures and funding patterns which will be shown by the evidence examined here, different sectors are often affected differently. This differential impact of central and local government policies forms an important part of the common and contrasting experiences of adults in the maintained, independent and voluntary strands of provision. And it is with a discussion of this that we begin.

Administrative responsibility for children

The most important differences between kinds of provision for young children stem from:

- the effects of being within or outside central and local government control;
- administrative location in different central and local government departments; and
- policy and practice between provision for different age-groups.

Location in the maintained or non-maintained sectors

The fact that there are two systems of provision for under-5s, within or outside central and local government control, stems from the

Table 3.1 Factors considered by leaders of playgroups to be most significant in constraining the development of an appropriate curriculum for young children (%)

Constraining factors	
Staff not trained for early years specialism	44.1
Inexperienced staff	51.6
Inadequate levels of staffing	62.4
Lack of opportunities for staff training and INSET	17.2
Poor monitoring of provision	18.3
Inappropriate procedures for assessing children	15.1
Inadequate provision for parental involvement	52.7
Restricted space for learning	43.0
Inappropriate accommodation	57.0
Limited opportunities for learning out of doors	12.9
Insufficient budget for resources	81.7
Poor management of the institution	36.6

Note: n=93.

historical development of preschool provision. Educational provision for the 3–5 age-group was a voluntary responsibility within the remit of local authorities before the Education Act 1944. But up to the beginning of the Second World War the development of provision was piecemeal and at a low level. The wartime nurseries which were provided to meet the care and education needs of children of women workers brought a short-term improvement in provision. They were, however, closed down in 1945 except for the small proportion of priority day nurseries. In exchange, the 1944 Act made 'nursery education' a permissive responsibility of local education authorities, to be expanded by each authority as funds and staff ratios in the compulsory sector allowed.

In the event, economic and political constraints meant that, even after the optimistic days of the 1972 White Paper (DES, 1972) in which Margaret Thatcher, as Secretary of State for Education, forecast a planned expansion, there was only a very slow and uneven growth in the number of places available. This failure to meet the demand for places in maintained nursery education left a gap which was filled between the 1960s and 1980s by a plethora of playgroups and nurseries provided by the voluntary and independent sectors and by community effort, while small numbers of children in this age-group also attended local authority day nurseries and combined education and social services nursery centres. As we saw in Chapter 2, the consequent inadequacies can be seen in the differences between the financial status and accommodation available to the voluntary sector (e.g. playgroups) and that available to maintained provision for children under 5.

Financial status and access to resources of course have an enormous impact not only on working conditions but also on approaches to planning and, indeed, the way in which the curriculum is conceived. And inevitably our evidence revealed this. Playgroup leaders, for example, gave 'Insufficient budget for resources' (81.7%) as by far the most significant factor constraining the quality of their provision.

However, there are deeper aspects of this which a further scrutiny of our data reveals. For, as can be seen from Table 3.1, the other factors which they rated highly as restraining the provision of an appropriate curriculum for young children were 'Inadequate levels of staffing' (62.4%), 'Inappropriate accommodation' (57%) and 'Inadequate provision for parental involvement' (52.7%). All these are the direct result of low levels of funding and resourcing in the voluntary sector.

We also saw in Chapter 1 at differential levels of funding between the different sectors of provision have a direct impact on the availability and use of accommodation. It was noted there that most types of provision were obliged to share accommodation. And this in itself is an indication of overall low levels of funding. However, we also saw there that playgroups (preschools), which are the major providers in the voluntary sector, share all aspects of their accommodation to a far greater extent than other forms of provision.

Table 3.2   Who shares with whom

The majority of playgroups (74.5%)	shared with primary schools, church groups and clubs, mother and toddler groups, and/or Sunday schools
Approximately a fifth of:	
• infant/first schools (23.3%)	• shared with junior/middle schools, playgroups and/or community groups
• special schools (18.6%)	• shared with hospitals, secondary schools, health authority units and/or community education units
• local authority day nurseries (19.1%)	• shared with playgroups, drop-ins for under-5s and/or social services
• independent nursery schools (20.8%)	• shared with church groups and clubs
About a tenth of:	
• primary schools (11.4%)	• shared with playgroups and/or adult education departments
• independent preparatory schools (9.8%)	• shared with nursery, junior and senior schools, and/or clubs
• private/workplace nurseries (13.9%)	• shared with church groups/clubs and/or Sunday schools
A small proportion of nursery schools (5.6%)	shared with infant schools, social services and/or parent support groups

Our further analysis also revealed some interesting details about who shares with whom (Table 3.2). In particular, this has revealed that playgroups (preschools) are faced with the necessity of establishing themselves in a wide range of settings, including schools, church halls and community centres. In contrast, schools, especially those catering for children of statutory school age, experience far greater security in this respect and, where they do share accommodation, do so with other educational institutions. However, it is clear that the issue of resourcing, as expressed through dissatisfaction with accommodation, is seen as having a significant impact on quality of provision in all types of setting except local authority day nurseries in the maintained sector (Table 3.3).

We also noted in Chapter 2 the extent to which levels of funding and resources affect policy and practice for different age phases, especially in terms of the provision of full- and part-time places for the under-5s (see Table 2.1) There is a further significance to this, and it reveals an important inadequacy in provision for 4-year-olds in the maintained sector. For, since the majority of non-statutory 4-year-olds in educational settings in England and Wales are enrolled in infant classes, that significant proportion is being deprived of the levels of provision which they might be receiving either in the independent sector or in state-maintained nursery schools and centres. There is thus an important mismatch here between the stated administrative intention and the real situation.

The second major source of differences in levels and forms of provision which we identified at the beginning of this chapter is the administrative location of the institution. For there are crucial

Table 3.3 Comparison of views on 'Inappropriate accommodation' across all early years provision (%)

	'Inappropriate accommodation' considered to be a highly significant constraining factor
Nursery schools	42.2
Infant/first schools	40.3
Primary schools	42.0
Special schools	41.7
Local authority day nurseries	9.5
Independent preparatory schools	49.2
Independent nursery schools	33.3
Private/workplace nurseries	35.3
Playgroups	57.0

differences which derive from the contrasting conditions created by the administrative arrangements, and even the legal requirements, which apply when provision is managed by either education or health or social services departments, at both local and national levels.

Administration by education or health/social services departments

Differences between the policies of different central and local government departments originate in the demarcation between the departments of central government with lead responsibility for children, the Department of Health (DH) (previously the Department of Health and Social Security) and the Department for Education and Employment (DfEE) (previously the Department of Education and Science).

In this policy division the following come under Health:

- Children cared for by childminders (most children under the age of 3).
- Children up to 5 in day nurseries, private nurseries, private nursery schools and preschools (playgroups).
- Play and out-of-school provision for children under 8.

The services under Education are as follows:

- Children of 3–8 in maintained education settings.
- Children of any age in independent schools, as long as there is a minimum of five children over the age of 5.

This demarcation was based on the assumption that it was not appropriate for children under the age of 3 to take part in group settings for educational provision, and that any group provision for them would be that required to protect them from the impact of damaging family circumstances. Since the end of the 1980s this division has been enshrined in two radical pieces of legislation, the Education Reform Act 1988 (DfEE) and the Children Act 1989 (DH), each affecting those settings within the remit of the relevant department.

This can be seen most clearly in the different ratios required for practitioners working with children in settings for which the two departments are responsible. For instance, as we saw in Chapter 2, the survey shows that in local authority day nurseries with children aged 3 and 4, the staff:child ratio is 1:4, whereas in local authority nursery schools, where the children are of the same age, the ratio is 1:13 (see Table 2.3). However, as we also saw in Chapter 2, the actual figure, in terms of the number of children for whom responsibility must be taken, can be twice this, where attendance is on a half-time basis. In non-maintained under-8s settings, which come under health and so-cial services departments, there is a slightly higher adult:child ratio than in state-maintained provision (1:7 versus 1:11).

Again, different assumptions by different central and local govern-ment departments show in the disposition of full- and part-time places. For, again as we saw in Chapter 2, the majority of children attending predominantly under-5s institutions are part time rather than full time, except those attending local authority day nurseries where the majority of children are full time. And this, as we have stressed several times, must place huge demands on the practitioners.

Policy and practice between provision for different age-groups

All the differences we have discussed so far have a wide influence on practitioners. However, of the three areas of influence which we iden-tified at the beginning of this chapter, identifying age-phase-related differences is the least straightforward, because policy developments have recently begun to erode previously accepted dividing lines.

In this chapter, provision for children under 8 is taken as falling roughly into the age phases birth to 3, 3–5 and 5–8 because major landmarks have in the past been formed by the predominance of health and social services provision for the under-3s, by the starting age for maintained nursery education and many playgroups at 3, and by statutory compulsory entry to infant education in the term follow-ing the child's fifth birthday.

However, these administrative landmarks have, in England and Wales, a variable relationship with the real experiences of children, their families and those practitioners who care for and educate them. This is largely due to an acceleration in the numbers of children admit-ted to reception and mixed infant classes in infant and primary schools since 1986. Indeed, in Wales, because of a range of influences, not least the difficulties of meeting the needs of children in rural areas, this development has an even longer history.

The effects of the increase in admission of 4-year-olds have been to extend informally the scope of infant education to children of barely 4 years old and upwards. This, in turn, has led to an increase in the proportion of children of 3 in maintained nursery schools and classes, and has caused playgroups (preschools) to admit increasing numbers of children as young as 2, in order to compensate for the loss of older children. And anecdotal evidence from private providers of nurseries suggests a similar but even more premature trend in the independent sector, with children being removed from nurseries at the age of 2 in order to begin a formal educational programme in private schools

Table 3.4 Comparison of views on 'Inadequate levels of staffing' across all early years provision (%)

	'Inadequate levels of staffing' considered to be a highly significant constraining factor
Nursery schools	65.6
Infant/first schools	77.8
Primary schools	62.5
Special schools	65.0
Local authority day nurseries	38.1
Independent preparatory schools	65.6
Independent nursery schools	58.3
Private/workplace nurseries	70.6
Playgroups	62.4

Thus, while it is the practice to discuss age phases within early childhood education as if they reflected clear-cut markers in policy and practice, this is not in fact the case.

However, it is important to state the belief of a majority of practitioners that distinctions between the age phases are meaningful. For children under 3 do have a greater dependence on a close and secure relationship with one person within the staff of any group setting, and children between 3 and 5 need higher staff:pupil ratios than children over 5. This belief is reflected in the Children Act 1989, where there is a much higher adult:child ratio for younger children – 1:3 for children up to 2, 1:4 for children from 2 to 3.

In fact, as an illustration of the different cultures of early childhood education that are being referred to here, ratios show up the complex issues which can underlie practitioners' responses and which should be taken into account in interpreting them. All respondents placed 'Inadequate levels of staffing' high on their list of constraints on the provision of an appropriate curriculum for young children, with the exception of day nurseries, whose position will be discussed below (Table 3.4).

Between the settings within DfEE's remit and governed by the terms of the Education Reform Act 1988 the ratios are considerably lower than for settings within the remit of DH and the Children Act. The high adult:child ratio continues, for settings within the remit of the Children Act, at 1:8 for children between 3 and 5 (Department of Health, 1991, p. 41). This includes schools and nurseries in the independent and voluntary sectors as long as the schools do not have five or more children of compulsory age on role. Yet in maintained education services for children under 8, lower ratios are taken for granted.

Table 3.5 Comparison of views on 'Inadequate levels of staffing' and 'Staff not trained for early years specialism' across all under-8s provision (%)

	'Inadequate levels of staffing' considered to be a highly significant constraining factor	'Staff not trained for early years specialism' considered to be a highly significant constraining factor
Nursery schools	65.6	73.1
Infant/first schools	77.8	58.3
Primary schools	62.5	56.8
Special schools	65.0	41.7
Local authority day nurseries	38.1	52.4
Independent preparatory schools	65.6	57.4
Independent nursery schools	58.3	50.0
Private/workplace Nurseries	70.6	44.1
Playgroups	62.4	44.1

In maintained nursery classes, the ratio is one trained teacher and one trained nursery nurse to 26 children (a slightly better ratio in nursery schools), while in reception classes there is no formal limit on the numbers of children one teacher may be responsible for single handed.

These lower ratios are justified because trained teachers (and, in nursery education, nursery nurses) are present with the children. By contrast, the *Guidance and Regulations* for the Children Act does not envisage regulations about the employment of trained teachers in services within its remit, stating only that 'the part time services of teachers trained to deal with the early years may be a valuable re-source in a day nursery' (Department of Health, 1991, p. 40). This means that, although the *Guidance and Regulations* for the Children Act can specify ratios and other conditions in provision coming within the remit of social services departments, including day nurseries, play-groups and private nurseries, conditions in maintained nursery provision and in reception classes are not controlled by this Act and can be varied with comparative ease.

The survey findings about levels of staffing and early years special-isms, then, must be interpreted in the light of these factors which regulate adult:child ratios in the different sectors and age phases. For what is seen as inadequate in one sector or age phase may be differently viewed in another because of these differences of context. It is likely, therefore, that respondents had different ratios in mind when they ranked inadequate staffing as a constraint on the quality of their provision, but this does not imply totally different standards. Rather, it is a reminder that responses should be considered as a whole rather than piecemeal if we are to get as near as possible to what experiences and thinking they represent. It is the case, for instance, as Table 3.5 shows, that some of those who ranked 'Inadequate levels of staffing' lower than other respondents (although all but one group ranked it relatively high) gave a higher rating to 'Staff not being trained for early years specialism' instead.

There are thus important differences in the administrative contexts of early educational provision. And these have a significant effect on practitioners who are working with young children in these many different settings. Before we can consider what our survey revealed in relation to these effects, it is important to seek to understand how such fundamental differences of circumstance and viewpoint came about. To do this, we need to explore the evolution of central government policy since the 1970s.

The evolution and impact of government policy on provision for children under 8

A consideration of the findings of this research about different circumstances and beliefs of practitioners must take account of past policy towards the different sectors of provision. It is only a quarter of a century since the government White Paper to which we referred earlier (DES, 1972) acknowledged the importance of early education and promised a massive expansion of provision in this sector. Indeed, this, along with a promise of similar increases in the provision of in-service training, constituted the prime justification for its title, *Education: A Framework for Expansion*. Neither of those expansive ambitions, however, was in the event realized, largely as a result of the economic difficulties following the rise in oil prices in the 1970s.

Over the last quarter of a century, therefore, pressure for improvements in services for children under 5 has been deflected by those economic difficulties, compounded by the unwillingness of successive governments to respond to pressures for an increase in the quality of all social services by raising levels of taxation. The emphasis in the policy of central government has been on self-help, and minimal funding, along with encouragement for personal initiative, has been regarded as the best option following the failure of promises to expand nursery education after 1972.

This is, for instance, shown in the multi-agency Sunningdale Conference of January 1976 which was called by David Owen, then Minister of State for Health at the Department of Health and Social Security, to consider the daycare issue. The concern which led to the calling of that conference shows that thinking had progressed since the closure of most of the wartime day nurseries in the late 1940s. However, the approach defined shows not only that concern but also the limits imposed from the outset: 'It [the conference] was held because we all know that the situation currently facing the 0–5 age group is deeply worrying and that if we do not take every opportunity to improve existing provision then a whole generation of children's futures could be unnecessarily blighted' (DHSS/DES, 1976, Foreword by David Owen, p. 1). On the other hand, 'The theme is 'low cost'; we did not meet to discuss the details, we want to grapple with the attainable' (*ibid.*). And one participant at Sunningdale commented, 'the cuts are being justified on economic grounds; but they also reflect political priorities' (*op.cit.*, p. 43).

In terms of policy, although collaboration between existing services was given high priority at the conference, very little real progress seems to have taken place at central government level since then. The picture at local level, however, is now somewhat different. Local development of strategies for co-ordinating services for children has been responsible for much improvement (Pugh and McQuail, 1996) and has to some extent offset the continuing and damaging competition among the different organizations and agencies for scarce resources.

If it may be said that the first governmental effect on early childhood practitioners has come about through a policy of non-intervention, the second, more recent, policy change has come through legislation in pursuit of major radical initiatives in education and in health and social services. The effects of these initiatives, however, are very different from, and indeed in conflict with, each other. For, whereas the substantial initiative embodied in the Children Act 1989 has reinforced and drawn together thinking about care and education in those sectors overseen by health and social services departments centrally and locally, the educational legislation has attempted a redirection of practitioners' thinking. Major legislation of the late 1980s, such as the Education Reform Act 1988, the National Curriculum and, since the survey was conducted, the *Desirable Outcomes for Children's Learning* (SCAA, 1996) before the age of compulsory school attendance, has radically altered the responsibilities of practitioners and providers, and has challenged practitioners to reconcile their old and new responsibilities. Signs of this effect on *infant* practitioners may be seen in their responses to the survey's request to prioritize factors they regard as influencing their professional development (Table 3.6). For, even in the context of the imposition of a subject-based National Curriculum, these responses highlight a felt need to develop their understanding of young children and the most

Table 3.6 Comparison among the under-8s provision in the ranking of the top five factors that are influential to the professional development of practitioners working with young children

Influential factors in professional development	Nursery schools	Infant schools	Primary schools	Special schools	Local authority day nurseries	Independent prep. schools	Independent nursery schools	Private and workplace nurseries	Playgroups
Knowledge of child development	1	1	1	1	1	1	1	1	1
Ability to assess individual children	2	3	3	2	2	2	3	3	2
Partnership with parents	3	4	5	4	4	5			3
Organizational skills	4	2	2	3	5	3	2	2	4
Openness to change	5	5		5	3		5	4	5
Meticulous planning			4			4	4		
Regular staff meetings								5	

effective ways of working with them, since they rank 'Knowledge of child development', 'Organizational skills' and 'Ability to assess individual children' as the three most important aspects of their professional development.

Similarly, there are lines of contrast running between groups of practitioners as a result of this legislation. The interests and needs of children up to the age of 8 have been asserted in terms of health, care and a curriculum that is developmentally appropriate under the Children Act. Yet, although this Act is the most recent piece of legislation, it does not affect maintained educational premises where staffing ratios and the curriculum are determined by existing practice and the Education Reform Act.

As may be expected from the discussion above, the settings available differ between the age phases. For children under 3, care is most often dependent on family care and childminders; some families employ or share nannies. This aspect of their lives is therefore not reflected in our survey and structured interviews. However, an increasing number of under-3s are in group care in the maintained, voluntary and independent sectors. Both private/workplace nurseries and playgroups also offer care and education for children under 3.

In the maintained health and social services sector, which has a long tradition of provision for children deemed to be in need or at risk, group settings continue to give high priority provision for a very small proportion of children defined as being in need of care, remedial help and custodial or 'place of safety' provision. Small numbers of babies, and somewhat larger numbers of toddlers and children under 3 are now also to be found in combined nursery centres where local authority education departments share responsibility with social services. Until very recently provision for under-3s in group settings has been defined primarily as care rather than education, and for children between 3 and 5 in day nurseries there has been a strong emphasis on providing for children's development and learning through play and social contact. Recent developments in both maintained and independent provision are questioning assumptions about the education of the under-3s, and parents too expect that their under-3s will receive education. Both points of view are represented in the survey and interview responses, although unfortunately the number of day nursery respondents was low (see Table 1.3).

The recent expansion of group care for children from birth to 3 years of age in voluntary and independent settings reflects the need of parents for affordable daycare. A few workplace nurseries existed in the 1970s and were regarded as a new development that gave cause for concern at that time (PPA, 1976). Now, there is a growing number of workplace nurseries catering in particular for children under 3 for whom maintained care is not an alternative option. A similar expansion of places in the independent sector is also a recent development; it was a negligible factor before 1985.

Among the full range of group settings available for under-3s, there may be a local mother and toddler club (not intended for daycare as its name makes clear), a day nursery (available only to those who can demonstrate that the child's, not the parent's, needs meet a definition of high priority), with a sliding scale for charges, a (fee-paying) playgroup that takes under-3s, a private nursery or a workplace nursery supported by the parent's employer. If the local authority has a combined nursery centre within reach, the parents may find the kind of flexible, affordable daycare with education they want from the child's babyhood until the start of compulsory school at 5, with a choice of provision during the full working day and during school holidays or shorter periods as wished. In most cases this will not be so, as the number of combined nursery centres is very small. One at least of the other forms of care will probably be available, with family members, friends and childminders filling in the gaps in care.

An important exception to this statement must be made, however. In rural areas the difficulties of finding suitable daycare provision are much greater even than those faced by urban families, and this must have an effect not just on the social experiences of young children but also on their parents' opportunities for work and for meeting other adults. This isolation is known to have a particularly powerful effect on the family if the parent is unsupported, and many rural education and other agencies make great efforts to provide at least visiting play opportunities during the week to enable children and parents to socialize. The factor of parent need in relation to the services available locally needs to be borne in mind when thinking of, for instance, the work of playgroup leaders and workers in rural areas, or day nursery staff in deprived urban communities with high unemployment.

For the 3–5-year-olds the same range of settings may be found, but again, not more than one or two locally. Playgroups or preschools cater for the majority of children under 5 years of age. An increasing number now offer full-day provision for children of working parents. Fees are charged, but efforts are made to keep places free for children in need where these are not sponsored by the local authority. The Preschool Learning Alliance, for example, has launched a fund-raising campaign to enable preschools to help more needy children and parents. In Wales, Welsh medium playgroups are provided by Mydiad Ysgolion Meithrin, which is independent of the Preschool Learning Alliance, as well as English language groups.

Places in private and workplace nurseries may be available locally, but the cost, even in a non-profit-making setting or when subsidized, is often prohibitive. It is not unusual for parents to withdraw children from a private nursery if a place in maintained nursery education or in a reception class is offered. If there is a maintained nursery school or class nearby, parents will probably be offered a part-time, free place (mornings or afternoons) with no after-school or holiday provision. As there are only places in nursery schools, centres and classes for about a quarter of 3- and 4 year-old children in England and Wales, it is likely that many will not have access to this form of provision. Others, whose parents work full time, will either not be able to use the provision or will have to combine it with other forms, perhaps going to a playgroup part time as well. This becomes even more complicated when the playgroup can only offer a place for some days in the week, not for all, which means that a third form of care and education is also needed. In the past, many working parents continued to employ childminders or to use private daycare because of the unhelpful hours offered by nursery schools and classes. It is thus hardly surprising that the majority take advantage of the chance of a full-time, free, place in an infant school reception class from the child's fourth birthday on.

As a result, preschools and playgroups as well as nursery schools and classes find that they are dealing increasingly with much younger children than before. Evidence from Wales about the experiences of 4-year-olds in reception classes (Davies, 1994) shows that parents, although initially pleased and hopeful of educational advantages for their children, often later say that they are not contented with the provision offered to such vulnerable children; they report behaviour disturbances and distress. This confirms research by Barrett (1986) which shows the stressful impact on new entrants to infant school of the demands made on them to conform to patterns of school organization and formal ways of learning. Davies also reports concern among Welsh reception teachers with 4-year-olds in their classes that they are not able to provide an appropriate curriculum, which increases the stress on the practitioners.

After entry to infant school the care and education of children between 5 and 8 is divided. Care before and after school and during holidays will depend on whether a voluntary group such as Kids' Clubs Network operates a service locally, or whether parents are able to employ a childminder or nanny to care for the child.

From the above discussion it will already be clear that there are many anomalies in the care and education of children under the age of 8. In fact, there are so many anomalies that it is easier to understand the distribution of services by thinking of many different approaches

Table 3.7 The difference in views among the under-8s provision in the order of importance given to the constraining factors, 'Staff not trained for early years specialism' and 'Inadequate levels of staffing', which are significant in the development of an appropriate curriculum for young children

	Nursery schools	Infant schools	Primary schools	Special schools	Local authority day nurseries	Independent prep. schools	Independent nursery schools	Private and workplace nurseries	Playgroups
Staff not trained for early years specialism	1	3	3	7	5	2	5	5	6
Inadequate levels of staffing	3	1	2	1	7	1	3	1	2

Note: Ranking order number shown is based on the percentages of respondents that have chosen the particular factor (i.e. 1 = chosen by the highest percentage.

coming together haphazardly within different areas and communities as a result of independent development, and being related to each other, if at all, through local attempts to co-ordinate efforts to provide services.

Thus, for parents, the factors which determine whether or not they can find the kind of care and education they want for their children are locally determined. This means that, nationally, parents and children experience a range of widely differing services, but at the family's own level this range is not usually available within the radius of their access.

In describing also the circumstances and beliefs of practitioners it is helpful to remember that the nature of their task is to some extent defined by the needs of their clientele. This, for example, is the only possible interpretation of the responses to our question concerning the relative significance of levels of staffing and the qualifications and training of staff (Table 3.7).

The impact of unco-ordinated development was deplored by a respondent from a local authority day nursery in London: 'Current *ad hoc* provision is often worse than nothing.' How *ad hoc* the development is at present may be seen especially in the financial status of different kinds of provision. The damaging effects of such exposure to chance become clearer as preliminary attempts are made to bring some kind of order to the provision available to under-5s and their parents, since over time the disparities will have, as we have seen, an impact on practitioners' attitudes to training and to educational processes themselves.

We now turn to a consideration of the impact of these events and policies on the attitudes and views of the practitioners as these were evidenced in both our survey and structured interviews.

Attitudes and views of practitioners

We should note at the outset that the attitudes and views we sought to obtain, both in the survey and the structured interviews were those of the most experienced practitioners – the heads of institutions. Further, it should be noted that a majority of these have worked professionally with young children for a considerable period of time, and have thus experienced the vicissitudes of changing policies which we have just delineated.

With this in mind, it is not surprising to find that one issue they continually highlight is that of staffing, not merely in terms of levels but also of quality of staffing. As we noted earlier, for example, practitioners in all sectors, except local authority day nurseries, ranked

Table 3.8 Comparison of views on parental partnership across all early years provision

	Overall ranking order given to the influential factor 'Partnership with parents' (1=most important)
Nursery schools	3
Infant/first schools	4
Primary schools	5
Special schools	4
Local authority day nurseries	4
Independent preparatory schools	5
Independent nursery schools	6
Private/workplace nurseries	6
Playgroups	3

'Inadequate levels of staffing' as a highly significant, and in some cases the most significant, factor constraining the provision of a high-quality curriculum for young children. But it is also important to set this particular finding against that indicating a wide concern with the importance of specialist training. Respondents from all sectors recorded this concern, but it is significant that those working in the education sector – headteachers in state-maintained and independent preparatory schools (by definition themselves trained and qualified teachers) – ranked it very highly (Table 3.7).

In addition to the issue of staffing, which has been highlighted throughout our discussion, there are other themes which emerge from the analysis of the data which relate directly to the administrative and political context we have described. The first of these is the ambivalent views which the practitioners have of their relationships with parents.

Views on partnerships with parents

In spite of all their differences of circumstance, the responses of heads of institutions showed a recognition that the task of the early childhood practitioner is made more complex because children of such a vulnerable age cannot be considered in isolation from their parents. When asked to rank factors which they regard as influential in the professional development of early years practitioners, 'Partnership with parents' was ranked by everyone as between third and sixth of the fifteen factors they were asked to consider (Table 3.8).

Within this, however, there are other interesting patterns to be discerned. For example, those working with younger children in the

ble 3.9 Comparison of teaching qualifications held by heads of maintained
d non-maintained under-8s institutions (%)

	State-maintained under-8s provisions	Non-maintained under-8s provisions
A(Ed)/BEd/BAdd	28.8	7.1
GCE	10.6	7.0
ert. Ed. (2 years)	11.7	8.6
ert. Ed. (3 years)	43.8	16.6

e concerned with relationships with parents as an essential founda-
ion for their work with children.

The foregoing discussion has indicated the variety of circumstances
and histories which those who work in settings for young children
bring to their work. This will be explored in depth in Chapter 4. This
variety is paralleled by the bewildering range of qualifications held by
these practitioners.

Attitudes to training and qualifications

The qualifications of practitioners working in the settings for children
up to the age of 8 have been outlined in broad terms in Chapter 2,
where we noted that early childhood care and education is a long way
from being a degreed profession. Indeed, we saw that the level of
initial qualification and take-up of award-bearing in-service opportunities were both comparatively low in the overall figures. We must
now extend our scrutiny to see if deeper patterns may be discerned
within this picture.

Our findings show some differentiation by levels of qualification
between the maintained and non-maintained sectors. The qualifications of heads, for example, show that those responsible for state-
maintained under-8s institutions are more likely to hold a BA(Ed)/
BEd or BAdd than heads of independent under-8 institutions (Table
3.9). The total, however is only 28% (compared with 7.1% in the independent sector). The same pattern emerges in relation to other teaching qualifications, such as specialist diplomas and taught masters'
degrees.

On the other hand, our evidence shows that heads in the maintained sector have no experience of working in the voluntary sector,
since none had playgroup qualifications. This contrasts significantly
with heads in the independent sector where more than 23% reported
that they had attended short courses organized by the PreSchool Playgroup Association (now the Preschool Learning Alliance) and had
been awarded the Diploma in Playgroup Practice.

maintained and voluntary sectors ranked this parti
compared to those working with older children. Perh̲
interesting, however, is the fact that it was considered l
in spite of the age of the children, by those working in
dent sector – in preparatory and independent nursery s
private workplace nurseries. This could be explained by
private providers are more likely to perceive parents as c
partners.

It is clear from the structured interviews as well as fror
that a range of interpretations is given to the purpose of
with parents, with educational aims becoming mo
focused in the replies of those working with the 5–8-year
titioners in all kinds of settings, however, experience th
ities of trying to provide for children's learning and deve
needs while having at the same time to be aware of and
their parents' needs for time to work, to have a break from
involved in bringing up children, and for personal suppo
task as parents, for which many feel they have not been pr
all.

This is a burden that falls especially upon practitioners
with children under 3 and their families, where relationships
parent and practitioner are normally closer than at later stages
of the child's dependency. Sometimes there are difficult con
tween the practitioner's view of the child's needs and of the
needs; sometimes supporting the child and supporting the p
well has to mean negotiations of great inter-personal sensitivit
titioners in local authority day nurseries, in particular, exp
much stress and a high rate of ill-health because of the high l
need of both children and parents. This may explain the low
return of questionnaires by day nurseries (12%), equal lowes
private and workplace nurseries.

Evidence of this conflict may be seen in the range of names
were discovered to represent local authority day nurseries, as we
in Chapter 1 (see Table 1.2). Some use the traditional term 'day
sery' or a more modern version of the same idea 'childcare cer
some imply a wider range of possibilities in calling themselves a
centre', 'children's centre' or 'young children's centre'; other na
imply approaches that are wider again, but still focused primarily
children, as in 'under-5s centre,' 'under-5s resource centre', 'under
education centre' or 'under-8s centre'; while some may have a speci
ist flavour as in 'nursery centre' or 'early years centre'. One nan
'family centre', specifically implies a commitment to the needs of fai
ilies, but there is no doubt that staff in all the centres and nurseries w

Those who head the institutions offering places to children under 3 across all provision or to those under 5 outside the maintained sector tended to have fewer first degree qualifications in education (BA(Ed)/ BEd/BAdd), with the notable exception of heads of independent preparatory schools with classes for under-5s attached.

We noted in Chapter 2 that none of the leaders of playgroups was without a qualification, and, indeed, that nearly two-thirds of them had more than one qualification. These qualifications are most likely to be, however, very short courses, such as the PPA Diploma in Playgroup Practice or other playgroup qualifications, all of which are low in grade, compared for example to a first degree. In fact, fewer than one in ten of heads working in the voluntary sector had a first degree, usually a degree in education. The status of the qualifications of heads of private and workplace nurseries were also at a lower level than first degree. These heads were mainly qualified through NNEB or City & Guilds courses. Just over one in twenty of them had first degrees, all of which were first degrees in education. And a further tenth were teachers who had qualified through a Certificate in Education.

Just over a quarter of heads of independent nursery schools had first degrees, but in this instance it was unlikely to be a first degree in education. More than a tenth were qualified by way of a Postgraduate Certificate in Education, and thus held first degrees in subjects other than education. Again, however, the majority were non-graduates who held either NNEB/City & Guilds or the two-year Certificate in Education, a qualification which, as was noted in Chapter 2, was abolished in 1960. A very high proportion of heads of private nursery schools – over 30% – held the Montessori Certificate, a qualification which was featured as a very significant qualification in this sector, although not in the others.

More than half the heads of independent preparatory schools held first degrees, of which the majority were in subjects other than education. The remaining heads in this sector were qualified through a Certificate in Education, and again a significant number of these – a fifth – held a two-year certificate.

The overall picture, therefore, although displaying slight, and perhaps significant, variations from sector to sector, is not impressive. The question which must be asked is whether what emerges as a general low level of qualifications is attributable to a lack of interest on the part of practitioners or to a lack of appropriate opportunities, especially for further study and professional development.

There is no doubt that lack of appropriate opportunities has played its part in the emergence of this picture. Most taught masters' courses in education, for example, have traditionally been aimed at teachers in the secondary sector and thus have rightly been seen as lacking in relevance to early years practitioners, and the same may be said of in-service BEd courses and many advanced certificate and diploma courses. It must also be acknowledged that for those practitioners who are not qualified teachers, perhaps most notable nursery nurses, there exists no clear career structure and, by implication, no routes to further training. Lack of appropriate opportunity, therefore, must certainly be recognized as a contributory factor here.

That lack of interest has played its part must also be conceded, however. For, as we saw in Chapter 2, this is reflected in the low ranking given by our respondents to the significance of such factors as 'Familiarity with recent research', 'Local authority-based in-service training', 'School-based in-service training', 'Access to professional journals' and 'Higher education-based in-service training' which were ranked as the least important influences on quality of provision (see Table 2.10).

This set of attitudes is oddly out of harmony with the views expressed by the practitioners concerning the key elements of a quality curriculum for the early years.

The views of practitioners about education in the early years

One of the ways in which we can get more insight into how these factors and practitioner's circumstances link with their different beliefs and practices is to consider in greater detail the responses to Questions 16–18, which followed the information sections of the questionaire. These questions, as we noted in Chapter 2, related to their beliefs about what a quality early years curriculum consists of, what are the factors which conduce to and constrain such a curriculum, and how good early years practitioners can be prepared.

This overview of practitioners' beliefs and insights begins with some quotations from the written and spoken comments from respondents as recorded in the survey (Questions 19 and 20) and in the structured interviews with heads of institutions participating in Phase Two of the research. These comments are used here to give a lively illustration of the ways in which practitioners articulated their beliefs, their insights from experience and their concerns about early childhood provision in England and Wales in the 1990s. They also introduce us to some of the dilemmas that preoccupy practitioners across the full range of group provision represented here, from the primary and preparatory school headteachers whose views introduce the discussion, to practitioners in maintained nursery education, in private nurseries and schools, in local authority day nurseries and in voluntary settings for under-5s.

These comments have the great advantages of the spontaneity and genuineness of the speaker's individual 'voice', personal qualities and professional experience. They hold invaluable information for all who care about early education and in Chapter 4 a full narrative analysis of the qualitative responses to the survey will draw out data about the deep levels of practitioners' thinking about the curriculum in the early years.

The coherence of the phase from birth to 8 is much debated by the practitioners in infant education, who are most affected by the National Curriculum, yet there is one distinctive quality of all children under the age of about 8 years old. They are dependent, in varying degrees according to their development, on adults for their physical, emotional, social, linguistic and cognitive development. They are not yet capable of surviving and thriving without close relationships with one or more adults. Although they become increasingly able to learn with and from other children and on their own, and benefit greatly from opportunities to do this, they need the structure and stimulus provided by secure relationships with particular known and trusted adults. The similarity between all children under 8 is far greater than the differences between the different age phases.

Respondents have shown that the vulnerability and dependence of children under 8 lead them to believe that the aims of education for children should include provision for children's learning across the whole of their personal development. As one head of a London preparatory school said about his view of the education of children under 8: 'I think actually we do teach them quite a lot that is important to them, but it is actually getting the person right in the early years that is very, very important.'

On the whole, the first impression from respondents' articulation of their beliefs is that they adhere strongly to a developmental approach where the child's personal growth and happiness are seen as the legitimation of educational provision. Here, there would seem to be little division. As the headteacher quoted above remarked, 'Life has got to appear to them to be full of excitement and praise'. He also mentioned the importance of children experiencing feelings of security, respect and trust for adults. But warning bells are sounded by other respondents. The head of an inner-London maintained primary school felt the tension between his belief in a developmental approach and a very different definition of education which has become extremely influential: 'I suppose these are terrible phrases nowadays to even mention, like child-centredness . . .'

There are clearly different cultures in conflict here, and this is communicated by respondents in terms of statements of belief about such aspects of their professional practice as, what quality means to them, a kind of broad expression of the central features of their pedagogy; how they conceptualize the early years curriculum; what constitutes quality in it; and how such quality can be achieved; and, underlying everything else, how they perceive the child.

As we saw in Chapter 2, respondents' answers to those parts of the questionnaire where they were invited to rank certain factors to do with quality in the early years curriculum in order of importance show that there is broad agreement overall on the need to give priority to children's developmental needs (see Table 2.9). This can be seen from the fact that the majority of heads of every type of group setting across all the different sectors thought that 'Knowledge of child development' was the most influential in professional development.

Yet this consensus should not obscure the diversity of ways of conceptualizing aims for the education of under-8s, and the responses to the questionnaire have shown that there are several strong cultures within the range of views represented.

Another primary school headteacher was forthright in expressing concern about the influence of the National Curriculum on practitioners who sought to implement a developmental approach to education in the early years. This was a particular worry because, in her view, each child has a culture of his or her own through which he or she apprehends the world and learns about it: 'It [the curriculum] has to be appropriate to those children . . . I think this is where the National Curriculum [for history and geography] has fallen down with younger children . . .' It would be inaccurate to conclude from this that an era of developmental approaches has been truncated by the arrival of the National Curriculum. Rather, it appears that practitioners have long been influenced by the pressure of several different interpretations of the role and nature of education in the early years, among which the developmental view has been one.

Further, the responses of practitioners have made it plain that there also exist different ways of interpreting developmental approaches. While some have tended towards fostering children's development in social, emotional, physical, linguistic and intellectual terms and have defined their curriculum accordingly, others have been working towards seeing child and practitioner as partners in learning and constructing understanding together. Others again have seen children as needing firm control and a thorough grounding in the basics of subjects they will encounter in later secondary school years, or have defined developmentally appropriate provision as giving equal access through a focus on children's own linguistic and cultural diversity as the starting-point for their learning. Puzzlingly, although understandably, some aspects of these different interpretations can be seen combined within any one practitioner's viewpoint.

Into this mixture of pressures the National Curriculum has come as an immediate requirement on those with responsibility for children over the age of compulsory school entry, and as a force to be reckoned with by those whose responsibility is for children under 5. Its requirements in terms of programmes of study (the content to be offered to children) have been less disruptive to practitioners than have the associated Attainment Targets, which demand performance within given levels by all children. The downward pressure of which some nursery education respondents have complained in their responses seems to have been caused by a kind of 'gatekeeper' role that under-5s practitioners perceived themselves as compelled into, in which their function is that of making sure that children reach a particular performance level whatever their starting-point. The 1996 'desirable outcomes' for children's learning before entry to compulsory schooling appear to confirm this diagnosis of respondents (SCAA, 1996).

A further analysis of some responses to Question 16 of the questionnaire, the invitation to rank in order some factors conducive to a quality curriculum, gives us some light on the ways in which the circumstances of practitioners' professional lives have a formative influence on their approaches to their professional tasks.

Of the sixteen factors listed (see Appendix B), five related directly to staff training and experience – qualifications and in-service training, range and length of experience and more general staff qualities – and it is interesting to note the differential responses we received from the different sectors of provision.

Table 3.10 Comparison of views on the importance of 'Qualifications of staff' across all early years provision (%)

	'Qualifications of staff' considered to be highly significant in supporting the development of an appropriate curriculum for young children
Nursery schools	51.1
Infant/first schools	23.6
Primary schools	26.1
Special schools	23.3
Local authority day nurseries	28.6
Independent preparatory schools	24.6
Independent nursery schools	16.7
Private/workplace nurseries	17.6
Playgroups	19.1

'Qualifications of staff' had a varying importance for certain groups of respondents (Table 3.10). Just over a quarter (25.6%) of the respondents from all under-8 settings considered it to be highly significant, and the combined London responses were at exactly this proportional level, 25.6% again. In the settings in the counties, a higher proportion (35.1%) of respondents ranked qualifications as of great importance. In all local authority day nurseries, the proportion was 28.6%, and from the London day nurseries it was 29.4% compared with 25.0% from the county day nurseries. For all playgroups the proportion was 19.1%, with a lower proportion by heads of London settings given by 15.3% compared with county playgroups given by 25.7%.

Overall, just under a third (31.4%) of the respondents from under-8s provision in the maintained sector rated qualifications to be highly significant (London maintained provision for under-8s 30.4%, county maintained provision for under-8s 28.8%). In the combined non-maintained provision for under-8s the proportion was 19.5% (London non-maintained 19.6%, county non-maintained 20.4%). These figures show the influence of the compulsory school sector and the maintained under-5s education provision.

By contrast, the factor 'Range of experience of staff' (Table 3.11) reveals that in some sectors respondents showed a greater appreciation of the role of experience in enabling practitioners to provide a quality curriculum. In general, a slightly lower proportion (27.8%) rated it to be of less significance than staff qualifications, but the non-maintained sector valued experience more highly than qualification. Overall, the proportion from maintained under-8s provision is at 18.9% and non-maintained at 38.8%. Respondents from all London

Table 3.11 Comparison of views on the importance of the 'Range of experience of staff' across all early years provision (%)

	'Range of experience of staff' considered highly significant in supporting the development of an appropriate curriculum for young children
Nursery schools	10.0
Infant/first schools	16.7
Primary schools	15.9
Special schools	28.3
Local authority day nurseries	23.8
Independent preparatory schools	36.1
Independent nursery schools	33.3
Private/workplace nurseries	41.2
Playgroups	44.7

Table 3.12 Comparison of views on the importance of the 'Length of experience of staff' across all early years provision (%)

	'Length of experience of staff' considered to be highly significant in supporting the development of an appropriate curriculum for young children
Nursery schools	1.1
Infant/first schools	1.4
Primary schools	4.5
Special schools	3.3
Local authority day nurseries	–
Independent preparatory schools	9.8
Independent nursery schools	25.0
Private/workplace nurseries	5.9
Playgroups	13.8

settings (26.3%) differed only slightly from those from those in the county settings (29.8%).

The most significant difference, however, was in the rating given to the range of experience of their staff by all the playgroup respondents. Overall, over two-fifths (44.7%) rated it as highly significant, with the proportion from London playgroups at 47.5%, and that from the counties at 40.0%. This contrasts significantly with local authority day nurseries, where overall the proportion was 23.8%, London settings 24.0% and county ones 25.0%. It is clear that, when higher-level qualifications are not available, judgements about the quality of staffing can only be made in relation to the extent and range of their experience.

Another factor which was explored, therefore, was the importance of 'Length of experience of staff' in the provision of a quality curriculum (Table 3.12). This was rated low when the overall responses are considered (given by only 7.2% of the respondents). However, in two sectors, the independent nursery schools and playgroups, the figures were significantly higher, probably for the reasons we have just suggested. This higher rating contrasts with the nil rating given by local authority day nurseries.

The most open factor relating to staff, 'Qualities of staff', elicited a high rating from all responses (74.2% of the respondents) (Table 3.13). This reinforced our conviction, which we indicated earlier has formed an underlying assumption of our research from the outset, that it is the quality of the practitioner which is the most crucial factor in determining the quality of provision.

However, although all gave a high rating to this as a general factor, there are significant differences in the ways in which quality was

Table 3.13   Comparison of views on the importance of 'Qualities of staff' across all early years provision (%)

	'Qualities of staff' considered to be highly significant in supporting the development of an appropriate curriculum for young children
Nursery schools	65.6
Infant/first schools	83.3
Primary schools	85.2
Special schools	78.3
Local authority day nurseries	61.9
Independent preparatory schools	91.8
Independent nursery schools	75.0
Private/workplace nurseries	61.8
Playgroups	64.9

Table 3.14   Comparison of views on the importance of 'Provision for staff development and INSET' across all early years provision (%)

	'Provision for staff development and INSET' considered to be significant in supporting the development of an appropriate curriculum for young children
Nursery schools	42.2
Infant/first schools	19.4
Primary schools	27.3
Special schools	43.3
Local authority day nurseries	57.1
Independent preparatory schools	8.2
Independent nursery schools	8.3
Private/workplace nurseries	14.7
Playgroups	7.4

perceived, as we have already noted in the differential responses to the importance of staff qualifications and experience.

In view of the high ranking given by all respondents to the general aspects of staffing quality, it is surprising to note the relatively low ranking given by many to the last of our five factors concerning staffing, 'Provision for staff development and INSET' (Table 3.14). It was seen as significant only by day nurseries, nursery schools and special schools in the maintained sector. All other sectors, including all forms of provision in the independent and voluntary sectors and institutions providing statutory provision in the maintained sector, ranked it low.

As was noted earlier, this must be disappointing for those who set store by continuous staff development, in-service education and

central issues of professional concern. However, a common de-nominator which can be identified is a conviction that in the early years, and certainly in the years prior to the age of statutory schooling, it is the child who must be the central focus of educational provision. As one playgroup leader expressed this, 'A child who is confident, independent, socially well integrated, has a good general knowledge and good physical co-ordination is far more important in the under-8s than a child who can speak French'. Another playgroup respondent felt that the time and money spent on organization and paperwork were an overwhelming and unnecessary burden on schools and teachers: 'Testing of the under-8s is futile and a waste of valuable money which should be channelled into schools themselves.' A prim-ary headteacher, however, felt that a distinction between the com-pulsory and precompulsory sectors has always been there but has been overlooked: 'The curriculum is obviously different for under-5s and over-5s – this needs to be clearly understood.'

In summary, this section of our survey evidence has revealed a consensus of views on broad issues concerning the curriculum. On some issues of detail, however, practitioners continue to disagree. These include the role of play in education, for example, fragmented and holistic approaches to curriculum content, competing models of curriculum, the relative merits of instruction and 'finding out'. The debate which has emerged from our research on all these major issues is explored in the 'practitioners' stories' which provide the basis for our narrative analysis in Chapter 4.

What has emerged from the research findings outlined in this chap-ter is the importance of maintaining an appropriately professional and intellectual context in which such discussion and debate can continue. For we need to be aware that not all influences on the early years curriculum are benign. And the least benign are those which would stifle discussion and debate. Changes at any level of education should be thought through most carefully, and should be open to continuous re-evaluation if we wish to improve the quality of our provision rather than freeze it in its present form or, worse, allow it to deteriorate.

4

From data collection to narrative insights: exploring practitioners' stories about quality and the early years curriculum

---

Our first published attempt to analyse the qualitative data from the PiP project (Whitehead, 1994) carried a warning – research produces 'stories' as well as facts and figures. Since then we have been agreeably surprised to find this outrageous notion supported in the most unlikely places. One of the academic 'cult' books of 1994, *The Bell Curve* (Hernstein and Murray), is a hard-nosed study of intelligence and race, written by a social scientist and a psychologist based at Harvard University. In the Preface to their book, the authors seek to wrap up their rather unpalatable message in a 'once upon a time' story about a great nation with two very different offspring and the dire consequences which lead to the tearing of the fragile web of civilization (*op.cit.*, pp. xxi–xxii). This is indeed purple prose and reminds us that even the most empirical and positivist of research traditions resorts to a good story when the going gets tough.

The discussion which follows is not a search for more strange bedfellows of this kind, but an attempt to deepen our understanding of the nature of the stories we have collected from our practitioner-researcher colleagues. This inevitably involves us in further reflections on the potential of narrative analysis in research, not just for generating purple prose, but for clarifying complex meanings.

Narrative, reflection on practice and professional development

Sorting out a large collection of stories and story fragments which surfaced in interviews and written responses to our questionnaire is a daunting task, but the stories are a large percentage of the material we have and we must honour them. Furthermore, this collection is of great significance because it is evidence of practitioners taking up the role of spectators of their own professional lives. This is a role which we regard as central to professional development.

For, at the heart of the general approach of the PiP project from the outset has been a clearly articulated decision to espouse the kind of research model which involves partnership with practitioners. This has involved us in exploring with them the everyday realities of their professional lives, in order to help them to make a difference to their practice. This approach is encapsulated in a classic definition as 'the study of a social situation with a view to improving the quality of action within it' (Elliott, 1991, p. 69). Otherwise known as 'action research', it provides a powerful answer to the need for a professionally responsive mode of inquiry which starts from the questions and dilemmas of practitioners and empowers them to set their own research agendas and determine their own provisional solutions. In the process of doing this, the practitioners at the sharp end articulate their insider knowledge, or expertise, including the ethical values and choices inherent in any social situation.

We think that we can play our part in 'making a difference' in early years settings by giving collegial support and the all-important good listener's ear to the stories of the practitioners who are undertaking the risky business of questioning their own practices and reworking them at the theoretical and the practical levels. We hope also to make academic research more responsive to professional needs in early years care and education by placing stories at the centre of our analysis, alongside the quantitative data. For this reason we gave practitioners ample opportunity to tell their stories both through the structured interviews (see Appendix A) and the later questions on the questionnaire (see Appendix B). It was the intention that the analysis of these 'stories' should provide a framework for the later analysis and evaluation of the data which would emerge from the action research case studies of Phase Two.

The sheer drama, complexity and richness of the social worlds found in early years settings can only be fully conveyed by narrative accounts. This is also true of other social settings where ordinary accounts turn out to be stories of survival, relationships and challenges in close-knit communities – schools, hospitals or kindergartens (Sacks, 1973; Jackson, 1979; Heath, 1983; Paley, 1992).

These international 'stories as evidence' are echoed in a current study of how early years teachers in New Zealand are making sense of the 'smorgasbord of theories to which they are exposed in the course of a lifetime' (May and Middleton, 1995, p.2). The analysis of these particular stories will be returned to in the following discussion, but it is important to note at this point that the New Zealand teachers were telling stories at a time of rapid, substantial and threatening change in the conditions of their professional lives.

Professional students of narrative claim that the form is all-pervasive and, therefore, has a part to play in every aspect of our lives. Furthermore, a powerful upsurge of narrative occurs when we are beset by major upheavals, by attacks on our self-identity, or subjected to tight social control (Cortazzi, 1994). It is well known that powerful stories are articulated by the survivors of accidents, disasters, internment and barbaric cruelty. While not trivializing these terrible testimonies, we note that the teachers in New Zealand were threatened by rapid changes in curriculum and public attitudes to education, changes over which they had little control. Experiences of loss of professional control and direction are not unknown to the practitioners we are working with in England and Wales.

It is all too easy to undervalue narratives of personal experience in cultures which have become obsessed with narrowly scientific notions about proof, evidence and absolute truth. Yet scientists of Nobel Prize stature, such as Karl Popper and Richard Feynman, have been a great deal less sure about 'proof' and 'definitions', and assert the importance of generating alternative and competing hypotheses (Popper, 1972; Feynman, 1988). We need to remind ourselves that the scientist's hypothesis is a type of possible story, or prediction, which is run up the flag-pole to be shot at!

Sorting out the stories

Stories, and the activity of narrating or telling them, suffer from their close association with lies ('telling tales'), fictions and the wild exaggeration of facts and truths. It is possible to make out a good case for the most bizarre stories, and this discussion will indicate the value of the fictive and the predictive stories used by early years professionals as they attempt to cope with change and upheaval, as well as the demands of research.

We have thus begun our analysis by attempting to group the stories we were told into three main categories.

'Just So' stories

Stories have always offered explanations about the way things are in a particular culture or social situation. Traditionally we label these kinds of stories myths, legends and folk tales. But, for the purposes of this discussion, we can borrow a useful term from Rudyard Kipling and name them 'Just So' Stories (Kipling, 1902). The bulk of the stories which our own and many other projects have collected (Grumet, 1990;

Gudmundsdottir, 1991) are narratives of self-identity and culture which ask 'Who are we?', 'How did we get here?', 'Where are we going?', 'What are our shared beliefs?'.

Attempts to sort out and answer such questions have a particularly high priority in periods of change, instability and cultural pluralism. Our own practitioners appear to be in the process of constantly re-defining, in quite explicit terms, what they take to be the nature of education, teaching and learning, and the early years curriculum: 'We believe that the adult facilitates the learning process by being fully involved with the children AT ALL TIMES. However, the adults must be sensitive in their judgement of when to intervene, question, explain, etc.' (nursery school headteacher, Berkshire). Our invitation to re-spondents to go further and tell us what they understood by *quality* in early years education led to many stories which transcended the ob-vious listing of facilities, materials and subjects: 'A quality curriculum should stimulate, challenge and excite but at the same time give space for practice and consolidation. It should create a well adjusted, moti-vated being with a positive learning attitude that will carry him or her through life' (nursery school headteacher, Devon). In these examples a narrative response has facilitated practitioner reflections on the nature of learning and the educational process. But 'Just So' stories about the quality curriculum are also based on some crucial assumptions about the nature of 'the child', often expressed in such terms as 'young children are naturally curious' or 'children, especially the younger ones, are egocentric and think in terms of "me" and "mine" '. All these explanatory stories suggested possible frameworks for the initial analysis of our qualitative data (Whitehead, 1994), and these will be returned to later in this section.

There is perhaps another urgent reason for early years practitioners to work on their own explanations of why and how things are the way they are. Their work with children involves them in constant explana-tions for their young learners about the 'why' and the 'how' of people, the world and the whole of life. Thus they must, as Gudmundsdottir (1991, p. 208) points out in respect of teachers, use narrative to solve the problem of translating 'knowing into telling'. Educators and carers are constantly telling children curriculum stories about famous people, literacy, science, history and mathematics, in homes and in group settings. At the same time, they are telling themselves stories about what they are doing with young children and why they are doing it. A central aim of action research is to make all these stories explicit and open to critical and creative analysis. This was precisely the aim also of the qualitative aspects of our survey and the structured interviews.

Porky pies

It is a strange irony of human experience that across all cultures and times we have debated, sought and honoured 'truth', while at the same time we have revered, protected and immortalized those purveyors of 'packs of lies' – the storytellers. One possible explanation of this paradox is that the ideal of 'truth' and the 'lies' of fiction are two sides of one coin. Stories are shared by cultures and told by individuals in order to try out possible versions of truth and reality (Gregory, 1977), but the 'over the top' variants offer a huge range of further possibilities.

Ideas about deception and lies are never simple and they vary within and across cultures, although all appear to give special licence to the tellers of tales if they are of the 'Just So' kind. An American ethnographer found that a fundamentalist Christian community, who regarded the stories of the Bible as revealed 'truth', strongly disapproved of the stories told in mainstream classrooms by teachers and published in school reading books (Heath, 1983). In this instance, the expectations of parents and teachers for the literacy development of the children were not easily co-ordinated. However, some of the children appeared to become biliteral and happily tolerated Henny-Penny in the classroom or playground and Joseph and his coat of many colours at home! But, however we place these kinds of stories on our scales of deception, they preserve important truths about the dangers of being naive and foolish, or the terrible extremes of sibling rivalry and parental favouritism.

Child developmentalists suggest that we cannot afford to underestimate the importance of infant and carer behaviours which may have been of evolutionary significance in the success of the human species (Bruner, 1976). This approach is concerned with play and the earliest communications between infants and their carers, but modern research is revealing that these kinds of interactions include surprising episodes of teasing and 'fibbing' initiated by playful babies (Reddy, 1991; Trevarthen, 1993). Facial and bodily signals are all-important in these games of 'I know that you know that I'm just kidding'. A smiling baby will close its eyes and pretend not to see a carer, or a spoonful of cereal; a giggling toddler will stand obviously in front of the washing-machine where she has hidden her shoes; adults will wink, or use an exaggerated tone of voice, as they tell a tall story. What is going on here and why does it start from birth and persist in cultures and individual lifetimes?

One answer may be that these playful deceptions create strong bonds of affection and pleasure between individuals. They build up a repertoire of private jokes and shared incidents which cement a relationship. They certainly keep infants and young children amused, intrigued and engaged with other people. Another explanation may be that little fibs help the child to get to grips with knowing and understanding that other people have minds and motives which can only be 'read' from signals and behaviours. So the porky pies are useful rehearsals for handling real deceptions, self-delusion, the 'otherness' of other people and the nature of truth and reality.

Some of our research stories are indicative of the practioners' struggles to reconcile conflicting principles in a period of unprecedented upheavals: 'We provide for the total learning experience rather than the fragmented or segmented areas of learning. Whilst maintaining a holistic approach and in an integrated way, we plan for, comply with and lay foundations for the earliest stages of the National Curriculum' (nursery school headteacher, North Yorkshire).

In the struggle to handle political as opposed to educational demands, some colleagues in early years settings have accommodated quite contradictory versions of the early years curriculum: 'All teachers are expected to deliver a broad and balanced curriculum, sensitive to the needs of individual children . . . It should prepare pupils for the opportunities, reponsibilities and experiences of adult life . . . All project work should include: maths, science, english, PE, RE, music, IT' (nursery school headteacher, Glamorgan).

Dangerous muddles and myths (EYCG, 1995) can only be dispelled by giving individuals the space and time to reflect on their full implications and reconstruct more useful and 'true to experience' hypotheses to run up the flag-pole. The partnerships between action researchers and research associates, which are the focus of the later phases of our project, aim to create both the space, and the trust and playfulness in which this creative reflection can occur.

Scheherazade's tales

The need to keep talking in order to save your life is a notion which permeates traditional and modern literature and folk psychology in most cultures (Bruner, 1990). Just as Sheherazade kept the stories coming in order to see another dawn, and Anansi, Brer Rabbit and Flossie came up with innumerable tales to ward off disaster (McKissack, 1986), so we all use stories as life-savers. This activity can be quite literally a way of hanging on to life at its most terrible, as in the stories of Anne Frank (1954) or Solzhenitsyn (1963). It can also be an important resource for all of us when we feel undervalued, hard-pressed and powerless, as many carers and early years practitioners testify in the stories they tell to researchers in many different parts of the world:

People are feeling 'I'm here for the children. I'm working for the kindergarten. To hell with the Government and the Association! To hell with everybody else!'. Some amazing teachers basically said, 'If they put one more thing on top of me, I'll walk away. I don't need it'. I've listened to these people who have said, 'I have had more migraines in the last 18 months than I've ever had'.

(May and Middleton, 1995, p. 5)

The stories in the qualitative data of the PiP project are inevitably, given the timing of our research, stories about 'hard times', and many can be analysed in terms of their Scheherazade function. Sometimes this is a form of 'whistling in the dark' until the good times return: 'With present economic cuts, and government attitudes and endemic changes to educational practice and philosophy, it is crucial to keep vision and commitment, based on knowledge and professionalism' (nursery school headteacher, Newham).

But it can also be a warning of worse things to come: 'Even though the response by the present Education Minister [John Patten] on behalf of the government devalues our work, it is important to support early years educators in their endeavours to continue explaining why it is important' (nursery school headteacher, Brent). There is a typically courageous early years response from many practitioners who tell of defending their principles and keeping the faith: 'It [a quality curriculum] will not be preparation for the National Curriculum; it will be giving children a positive and strong foundation for their future, as well as setting stimulating and enjoyable challenges in their present experience of learning' (nursery school headteacher, Waltham Forest).

Different as these stories are, then, they can all be seen as important strategies for reflecting on practice and as offering a platform from which practice may be understood and developed. It is also clear that this process of reflection through the adoption of a spectator role in relation to one's practice increases significantly in importance at times of extensive change in policies.

James Britton (1992) developed this notion of the spectator role in relation to everyday gossip and narratives of personal experience, as well as storytelling and literature. He pinned down its essential nature as the use of language for reflecting on the business of being and becoming (*op. cit.*, p. 125). Nothing could be more central to the lives and work of early years practitioners who are themselves living through a period of change and upheaval while also supporting young and vulnerable children as they struggle to be and to become.

Narrative frames for managing complexity

As was outlined earlier, the stories discussed in this chapter were not elicited by straightforward requests to 'tell us a story'. They occur as embedded narrative fragments in professional discussions and in response to research interviews and questionnaires. So they are always part of a broader context and other kinds of discourses, like the stories which are told in interviews (Nias, 1985; Huberman, 1993), over a family meal (Polanyi, 1985; Blum-Kulka, 1993) or in the presleep chatter of very young children (Weir, 1962; Nelson, 1989; Fox, 1993).

In this kind of data, the shapely folk structure of Labov's (Labov and Valetsky, 1967) New York City stories of life-threatening events and narrow ecapes is rare. The clear orientations, complications, evaluations and resolutions of such tales may not be obvious in our stories, but what we will find are the same assumptions which underpin all storytelling – namely, that it is central to human experience, that it shapes the meanings we impose on random happenings, and that it links us with our communities and cultures. Furthermore, everyday narratives are manifestations of the models constructed by the mind in order to handle compexity (Chafe, 1990), and practitioners' narratives about early learning should provide evidence of their own internal models of the learning and teaching process.

A start can be made on analysing our narrative fragments using a linguistic approach which was originally devised for exploring the universal features of folk tales (Propp, 1968). This suggests that their form and content can be charted as two intersecting axes of narrative. The horizontal story line is formed by telling, or writing, about events sequenced in temporal order, and is the best-known definition of a story. It is the 'and then . . . , and then . . . ' staple of every storyteller, from Chaucer to the emergent writer of 'news' in the infant classroom, and most of us recognize it when we meet it. But narrative also has a hidden, yet crucial, vertical structure which carries all the possibilities from which storytellers make choices, or judgements, about the similarities and differences between events, characters and places.

In the narratives found in research data, the key to understanding the assumptions and the values of the tellers can be located in their vertical choices. These include choices of words, events, protagonists and recurring metaphors (Eisner, 1985). Metaphors and these other story choices are powerful indicators of both the 'hidden' and the formal agendas of the social settings which produce them, as well as invaluable guides to self-knowledge and systematic self-study. The complexity and richness of interpretation made possible by these intersecting choices is not a blurring of the sharp focus of research but a remarkably sensitive indicator of fine-grained cultural, social and personal differences.

Investigating the vertical axes of narratives is the main concern of narrative research, but it can be done in varying degrees of depth and detail. This may be thought of as rather like the methods of the archaeologist who digs and sifts through layers of deposits. By focusing on the narrative choices and metaphors in our initial analysis of the stories we identified some key values and assumptions of our practitioners. These first excavations identified a layer of stories – stories about the early years curriculum, stories about the nature of children and stories about quality in early years education. As we saw in Chapter 3, there are differing views expressed within all these categories, as well as some areas of consensus, but the stories do confirm that practitioners are always acting from a theory of some kind. Research which has looked at the practice of early years teachers indicates that theory can be habitual, following a rule, or explicitly worked out, but it is 'unconsciously or consciously selected from a repertoire of strategies which are discursively, biographically, historically and culturally constructed' (May and Middleton, 1995, p. 2). Looking back at our first analysis, it is now much easier for us to identify these complex personal, social, historical and cultural constructs.

Stories about the early years curriculum

A curriculum is an act of narrative. It is a way of telling our children the story, or stories, of our culture – a selective account of those achievements, beliefs and skills which are far too important to be forgotten or left to chance. In this way we pass on the cultural and cognitive tools which are deemed essential to survival.

Lists

A simple list of the 'who' and the 'what' to include in a curriculum occurs in many of the stories told to the project. This is typical of all inventories, from the Doomsday Book to more recent documents such as those defining the statutory National Curriculum in maintained schools.

For example, we found a marked tendency for the independent sector practitioners to use traditional subject lists: 'language, reading, mathematics, science, history, geography, religious education, art, craft, design and technology, music, drama and speech, physical education, French, information technology' (independent preparatory school headteacher, Home Counties). The lists vary slightly, with English frequently replacing language, and some focus on 'Famous People' in order to cover history, geography and art. One questionnaire response asserts that 4- and 5-year-olds will 'do' Alexander Graham Bell, Isambard Kingdom Brunel, Augustus Welby Pugin, Pissaro, Leonardo da Vinci and Holbein in the next academic year (independent preparatory school headteacher, London).

The historical and cultural stories and assumptions behind these particular lists are fairly clear. With the exception of a couple of late twentieth-century newcomers, these are tales deeply rooted in the nineteenth century and in an education deemed appropriate for male leaders and shapers of a socially stratified Britain.

The narrators of these lists frequently make explicit the value judgements which shape their choices, and refer to their emphasis on 'traditional values: reading, writing, arithmetic' (independent preparatory school headteacher, London). These independent sector practitioners can be expected to be very conscious of the choices they are making because they do have a choice, since they are not legally bound by the National Curriculum selection of curriculum content.

However, other practitioners who enjoyed a similar freedom at the time, those in maintained nursery schools, were overwhelmingly in favour of a very different curriculum story and contributed to one of the project's main findings, that a broad curriculum based on the principles and implications of child development is preferable to a subject-based approach.

Lists were also much in evidence in infant schools and departments in the maintained sector, but they drew on a different cultural story from the lists given above. They reflected a dividing up of the significant resources to be passed on into packages of human inquiry and distinctive learning experiences. Thus this approach creates lists of the following kind: linguistic and literary, mathematical, artistic and creative, physical, scientific and technological, moral, spiritual, human and social. These categories are based on guidelines offered in the past by HMI (DES, 1977; 1985) and by local education authorities (for example, ILEA, 1987). The superficial similarities of these lists should not be allowed to obscure the fundamentally different assumptions they embody at the metaphoric level. The traditional lists of school subjects are ready-made tools which are handed down, with the obligation that they be accepted and used regardless of changing times and needs. The lists of areas of experience and distinctive learning are more like self-assembly kits and sets of adaptable tools which the learner will have to construct and modify appropriately.

Making sense
There is a view of the early years curriculum which emphasizes all the learning opportunities in a setting, all the behaviour that is

encouraged or discouraged, the routines and organization, and the ways in which all the adults interact with children and each other (EYCG, 1992). This view was informing the curriculum narratives told by most of the maintained sector nursery practitioners mentioned above, and it occurred across all the early years settings, including the independent sector. It was also noticeable in special schools' responses where there was an absence of lists of traditional subjects.

Three characteristics of this particular curriculum narrative began to emerge. First, this early years curriculum has highly flexible and permeable boundaries, or, as its tellers would say, it is by definition crosscurricular. Second, it is broad and balanced. And, third, it is a set of procedures for making sense of the world.

Many early years practitioners argue that the best way of supporting young children's learning is through this broad, crosscurricular and sense-making approach: 'allowing choice, the opportunity to express ideas, share thoughts, make decisions, make discoveries, to be able to explore and engage in real experiences' (special school headteacher, Hampshire). The ideal curriculum, according to many of these practitioners, is one which supports young children as they seek to make sense of the world in all its complexity, and never loses sight of the fact that 'in developing a quality curriculum for young children a teacher must always remember that the intellectual capacity of the child is considerably greater than the skills and capacities he or she possesses' (independent preparatory school headteacher, London).

This emerging concern with children's potential led many of our respondents to articulate their views on the nature of children and childhood.

Stories about children

The central character in all the responses we gathered was 'the child'. Even the more subject-oriented practitioners had a clear focus on the recipients of their teaching, while those who called themselves 'child-centred' lived up to their label.

Highly generalized notions about 'the child' do have limited usefulness – for instance, when we need to discuss theories and policies. This is fine, so long as we do not confuse 'the child', which is a particular historical and cultural construction, with the real children who arrive at the doors of early years settings. Later phases of this project will be totally focused on individual children and practitioners, but our first sweep analysis revealed underlying stories about three very persistent versions of 'the child'. These narrative constructions about children have portrayed them, in roughly historical order, as creatures of original sin; as endangered innocents; and as young scientists-cum-research partners.

Sinners

It seems rather extreme to claim that a puritanical belief in the innate wickedness of little children still exists among early years practitioners, but a number of our respondents choose metaphors and words which signal the survival of this view of the child: 'the training of young children is part of their development as redeemed children' (independent preparatory school principal, Kent).

While this is an unusually explicit formulation of the sinner story, there is a very widespread assumption that professional carers and educators must keep little children 'busy' – an assumption which is not unrelated to the folk wisdom that the devil will always find mischief for idle hands to do! A few stories in the data link quite explicitly personal cleanliness, good manners, shiny shoes, speaking 'decently' and keeping busy with bringing 'respect back to society'. In some independent schools this decency and busyness is ensured by a dizzying round of extracurricular activities – French, swimming, riding, playing musical instruments, judo and so on. Some early years workers in a maintained sector nursery school in London also attributed the challenges of their professional lives to the wicked families they had to work with, although their Headteacher challenged this underlying myth of innate evil: 'Another comment recently was, "You know we don't seem to have those terrible children we used to have". Well, I don't think the quality of the children has changed. I think it's what they're being offered is more interesting so they're not bored, so they're not behaving badly.'

Innocents

In the history of notions of childhood, the child of sin was replaced by the innocent cherub, 'trailing clouds of glory' (William Wordsworth). One of our respondents expressed this still influential story in terms of the need to value 'that of God' in everyone: 'You've got to look at what every child has in them and draw that out, give the child the praise for that and that usually has an enormously beneficial effect across the child's self-esteem and therefore across their performance' (independent preparatory school headteacher, London).

This belief in the innate goodness and innocence of the young child permeates the majority of the stories in our data and is signalled by the many references to ensuring the happines and security of the child. But the poet of 'clouds of glory' also warned that 'shades of the prison-house begin to close' around the growing child exposed to the corrupting influences of society. Hence the early years founding tradition of rescue and care which is well represented in these stories: 'There was this place, this sanctuary really of green and beauty and flowers, but I still think that happens every time I open the gates' (nursery school headteacher, London). Here we have the power of the enduring myth of the secret garden voiced by a contemporary educator. It is a reminder of the garden of paradise, the sanctuary of beauty and innocence, the 'Garten' of 'Kinder' in the middle of a corrupt and degrading city.

This care and rescue metaphor seems to have permeated the 'special educational needs' sector and appears in the stories we collected about young and vulnerable children and devoted practitioners who, in their words, bring the children the 'good news' of the 'adventure' of learning.

Scientists

A more recent conception of 'the child' was expressed in the stories of many practitioners across the full range of settings surveyed. This view comes through in descriptions of the curriculum as characterized by 'active involvement of children in constructing their knowledge through first-hand experience' (special school headteacher). The narrative here springs from psychological and linguistic studies of the cultural and social nature of human learning (Vygotsky, 1986; Bennett, 1993). It is a story about children constructing knowledge in partnership with their significant adults, both their personal and their professional carers and educators. The fragments of narrative from many of our respondents hint at this sophisticated notion of the child who is not a blank slate – 'Provide an environment where the children have the opportunity to be planners and builders of their own development' (infant school headteacher, London) – nor a rescued innocent – 'There's a lot more work involved in setting up a really interesting challenging environment than just plonking out puzzles and colouring' (nursery school headteacher, London) – nor a born sinner.

This respect for children's abilities as thinkers is expressed in curriculum terms as 'A quality curriculum is a liberal curriculum with provision for developing lateral thinking' (independent preparatory school, head of junior school, London).

Stories about quality

This issue of what constitutes a quality curriculum for the early years is of course a major focus of our research. And here again there are important stories to be interpreted.

Qualified practitioners

Stories about quality in the data are overwhelmingly tales about the importance in early years settings of highly qualified, professionally trained and committed practitioners. In the words of one primary practitioner, 'I find it difficult to keep separate the quality of the curriculum from the quality of the teacher'. And the story is more fully elaborated by a nursery headteacher: 'I think you need to be very thoughtful. I think you need to be able to reflect on what you're doing and have a forum to discuss that . . .' This head goes on to talk about liking children and keeping detailed records about them: 'If I were to cover up the name of the child there, the child would leap out of the page in all her kind of interest and excitement.'

Individual children

A concern with the unique child is another area of broad agreement, and even the need for high-quality professional training is expressed in terms of young children's needs and the practitioners' ability to identify and respond appropriately to these. Nursery school professionals are particularly strong in their view that child development should be central to the training of all under-8s workers. The key phrases surface again and again:

- 'value every child'
- 'develop the whole child'
- 'take account of all the child's needs, not just academic'
- 'provide child-centred high-quality learning experiences'
- 'create awareness of the child's present stage of learning'.

Teaching as art

Another kind of story about quality emerged from one of the pilot action research studies of the First Phase of the project. A group of early years practitioners in a London primary school taped their discussions of what they identified as the 'art' of caring and teaching. They rejected a view of this as simply a technician's job in which transmitting prescribed information and checking on its reception by passive pupils was all that was required. In their conversations they narrate stories about the essentially creative nature of their work, what one described as 'your special bit', when their own interests and enthusiasms are shared with the children. The same practitioner gave the project an interesting and haunting metaphor for education: 'an overall blanket thing that settles down on children.'

That this gentle, enveloping image is a far cry from smothering children's creative initiatives was confirmed by the group's conclusion about the complexity of their professional task which was centred on 'making them [the children] into creative people who can generalize from their experiences and work things out' (primary and nursery school staff, London).

Partnership with parents

The notion of a worthwhile partnership with parents and the school community is another dimension of quality as recorded in the stories in the data. As we saw in Chapter 3, it is almost exclusively focused on by practitioners in the maintained sector. We suggested there that one explanation of an apparent lack of concern with this factor in the independent sector might be found in a perception of parents as clients rather than as partners. We should not forget, however, that private and independent providers may well take it for granted that the paying customer calls the tune. One nursery headteacher expresses the maintained view with great clarity:

> We first want to establish very much a partnership ideal, that the parents know that we are there for their child, so that's our over-riding aim and it's very important. I feel very much that we have to be the ambassadors for the educational service, so it's very important that we get it right

This is the authentic professional voice, always seeing beyond the technicalities of simply getting by in the present, and valuing involvement with young children as part of an intention to improve the quality of life for them and their families.

It should come as no surprise to learn that our second look at the qualitative data indicates that the one overwhelming recommendation for *improving* the quality of early years education, put forward by respondents to the questionnaire, is 'universal nursery education for all under-5s'.

Returning to the data

Counting is not enough

We have now returned to a second-level analysis of the qualitative repsonses elicited by our questionnaire survey. Although this scrutiny is still in progress, we are increasingly aware of the importance of subjecting our complex data to subtle analysis and of resisting the desire to keep the task easy. Hence the assertion that simply counting responses and tallying occurrences is not enough. Of course, some kind of tallying does help as an initial indicator of the frequency of responses, as was shown in Chapter 2, but this is complicated in our research by the fact that our individual respondents are usually articulating a whole range of views, some of them quite contradictory, as indicated above. In addition to this surface level of statements, there are also clues hinting at the existence of deeper strata of attitudes and beliefs. Our qualitative data is not just rich data; it is dense – in the most complimentary sense of that term! For these reasons we committed ourselves at an early stage in the research to accepting that stories from early years practitioners must be treated as stories and that we must evolve our own kind of narrative analysis.

The business of narrative analysis is no more straightforward than anything else in research into human beliefs, behaviours and activities in social settings. We are aware of the expanding range of narrative models available to the researcher, including the sociological, psychological, anthropological and literary (Cortazzi, 1993), and we are evolving an approach which is within a literary tradition but not averse to using the insights of the other approaches.

We are currently doing two things. First, we are sorting our stories into broad categories which indicate that 'this story is about . . .'. Second, we are trying to penetrate the surfaces of the stories and unpick the threads of 'choices made' and the layering of motives. Currently, we are scrutinizing the responses of the three final questions in our national survey (see Appendix B):

- How would you describe a quality curriculum for young children?
- What improvements would you like to see in the current educational provision for under-8s?
- What improvements would you like to see in the current educational provision for professional training and development for practitioners who work with young children?

This second sweep analysis has two stages. There is a first scrutiny which involves reading and categorizing the themes of the stories in considerable detail. This also makes it possible to go on to study the exact words of the respondents in order to make a start on getting beneath the surfaces of their stories. In the second stage we will be searching the data with the aid of qualitative analysis software. Our pilot work with this highly sophisticated electronic tool for searching data indicates that the equally sophisticated judgements of the expert insider who knows early years settings is still required in order to initiate, interpret and make sense of the machine's counts and classifications.

Stories and themes

We have identified more than twenty different themes in our stories about the quality early years curriculum, but for the purposes of this discussion we are suggesting that these can be grouped into four major stories, plus a handful of significant minor tales.

Major stories – kinds of curricula

We are not averse to quantifying research responses whenever this is appropriate, and our four major stories are here presented in order of their occurrence and domination of the data. We can confirm our earlier published findings (Whitehead, 1994), discussed above, that three different stories about the nature of the early years curriculum dominate the data. Furthermore, one particular version is overwhelmingly popular and can be summarized as a narrative about a developmental curriculum (Blenkin and Kelly, 1996). This tells of a curriculum which is sensitive to young children's ages and stages of development – a story clearly articulated in the detailed submission from one infant school: 'Children bring varying experiences, expectations and abilities to school. They have differing needs. Children are individuals who learn at different rates. Children learn best with a progression of practical experiences. Children learn best when they are closely matched to the task and when appropriate expectations are placed upon them' (infant school headteacher, Hampshire).

A developmentally appropriate curriculum is focused on the individual learner's potential, requiring practitioners 'to put into practice individual programmes of learning to allow children to experience a sense of achievement – then time to build on/consolidate – until they become autonomous learners . . . To value the child as a learner, without undue reference to chronological age . . .' (independent preparatory school headteacher, London). This approach emphasizes the educative value of first-hand experiences of many kinds: 'Where are the opportunities to dam a gutter and cause a flood; to play snowballs and create ice particles by pressure; to observe the changing seasons; to experience the variety of products displayed in shops?' (independent preparatory school principal, London).

Comments of this kind indicate the distinctive investment in the pleasure and excitement of learning associated with this conception of curriculum: 'Learning should be an enjoyable experience'(infant school headteacher, London). And this pleasure may last a lifetime: 'To provide a lasting "glow" at the start of every child's education which may allow them to acquire the skills, motivation and abilities to sustain a mature development and provide them with the self-esteem to survive the experiences of adulthood' (infant school acting headteacher, Norfolk). 'Surviving the experiences of adulthood' is a telling phrase and indicates that behind this particular curriculum story is another 'romantic' tale about the child as endangered innocent, already doomed to enter the dark prison-house of adult experience (see above).

Our second curriculum story is also popular and described in terms of areas of experience, or of inquiry, labelled by the adjectives which best describe the activities involved: 'linguistic and literary, mathematical, aesthetic and creative, physical, scientific and technological, human and social, moral, spiritual' (infant school headteacher, London). These areas constitute a curriculum which is varied, broad and stimulating: 'The curriculum should be broad and enriching; provide differentiation and offer open-ended situations which extend learning. The National Curriculum should be integrated into existing good practice which recognizes that children come to school with a variety of experiences and an already increasing understanding of their environment' (infant school headteacher, Norfolk).

A comparatively small number of respondents tell a third curriculum story which is focused on teaching subjects and structuring the day in a traditional way: 'The three Rs in the morning. History/geography/ science (done as integrated project work in our school). PE, art and craft (usually related to the project work), recorded BBC and ITV television programmes, music and silent reading in the afternoon' (independent preparatory school headteacher, Buckinghamshire).

There is another traditional subtext here: the afternoon is a no-go area for the intellectual rigours of the three Rs, history, geography and science because, the story goes, young brains are at their freshest in the morning. Furthermore, PE, the arts and reading have far less intellectual content.

The mastery of basic skills is emphasized in this group of stories: 'Basic skills of number and letter recognition, saying and writing are repeated using a variety of situations. This to be followed, as and when the child is ready, by progress on to reading, writing words and number work' (independent preparatory school headteacher, London) – and there is a concern for structured learning, 'where the children are given structured instruction. A programme of learning with a formal approach . . .' (independent preparatory school deputy headteacher, Berkshire).

Although our, inevitably selective, examples of quotations from the stories about the three versions of a quality curriculum may not be representative of every sector of provision, our evidence revealed that all three versions are to be identified somewhere in all the types of settings we surveyed. In short, there is no direct relationship between sector – voluntary, independent or maintained – and curriculum story.

Major stories – activities and processes
A handful of our respondents (10 out of 542), mainly in state nursery

schools and special schools, refer specifically to a 'hidden curriculum'. They consider this to be of great significance because it creates the ethos of an early years setting, namely, the emotional and social processes at work in any group situation: 'In the early years it is not possible to separate children's learning experience from their need for care and support. The 'hidden curriculum' is as important as the published curriculum as we aim to encourage independence, self-motivation, autonomy and a caring attitude to others' (nursery school headteacher, London).

These minority claims about a 'hidden curriculum' are used here to introduce a large group of stories which we have loosely categorized as narratives about the distinctive activities and complex features associated with a quality early years curriculum. In a sense these stories of un-timetabled but persuasive processes, features and activities do constitute a hidden curriculum, although the majority sees these as salient and not 'hidden' aspects. The really big story from all the early years settings surveyed is about the creation of an appropriate learning environment. This concern with the environment starts with the setting, inside and outside: 'A well resourced learning environment including both indoor and outdoor areas which enables children to have access to a broad range of equipment and materials' (nursery school headteacher, London).

Many practitioners go on to identify the potential of the learning environment just beyond the boundaries of the settings and advocate walks in local streets, parks and countryside, as well as visits to museums and galleries. The issue of resources and material provision required to create a 'visually attractive and intellectually stimulating' environment (North Tyneside infant school headteacher) is raised by all the respondents.

A Buckinghamshire nursery headteacher summarizes the importance for the early years of a planned learning environment: 'an enabling environment where the children can explore their own enthusiasms; a developing environment to expand experience; an imaginative environment to promote the discovery of new enthusiasms.'

If we can identify a big story about early years settings as created learning environments, we can also identify a big story about the significance of children's play in these environments. All our respondents, across the settings, tell us that children need 'opportunities to learn by play and discovery' (London preparatory school headteacher). The headteacher of a London nursery school provided one of the longest and most lucidly argued accounts of a quality curriculum for young children which included these comments on play: 'The most appropriate way to teach and for children to learn is through PLAY – planned and structured in such a way that children delight in learning which becomes purposeful and more a way of thinking, seeing and doing, rather than subjects that have to be learned.'

Fewer types of settings appeared to apply these notions about play and learning to the outside areas available: outdoor play was only focused on by practitioners in day nurseries, nursery schools and special schools. The case for outdoor play was again put by the respondent cited above, as was the possible reason for our limited data on this topic: 'Many classes do not have free access to an outdoor play area and children are expected to "play out" in barren playgrounds and spend long lunch hours with little play equipment and large numbers of older children.'

There is a low frequency of practitioner stories about cultural pluralism, equal opportunities policies and multicultural education from all the settings, and none from one – the independent preparatory schools. This latter echoes the finding we reported in Chapter 2, that a vast majority of bilingual young children were located in the maintained sector and especially in nursery school provision, with only a very small proportion to be found in the independent sector. We explained this there in terms of local authority policy, provision and need, suggesting that it might reflect the policy of many local authorities and other providers in the maintained sector to direct resources towards young children who are at the beginning stages of learning English during this critical period of early childhood. This omission may also be interpreted, from the perspective of the private sector, in terms of the social 'open Sesame' which this sector provides for those who desire total assimilation into the British middle-class establishment.

Conversely, in many of the nursery schools a quality curriculum is expected to 'reflect the diversity of the community young children are growing up in '(London), while the approach to equal opportunities is one 'which can be seen in action'(London nursery school headteacher). There is a clearly expressed view that the nurturing of children's own self-esteem will be crucial to the development of respect for others and form the foundation of the setting's multicultural perspective. A conception of an education for democracy underpins some of these curriculum-defining stories: 'A curriculum that, with adequate resourcing in human and material terms, allows each child to develop and grow into a full participating member of society' (Nottingham infant school headteacher).

A thin scatter of respondents highlight the role of a quality curriculum in establishing traditional social skills and clear moral training: 'emphasis upon social skills, where discipline, courtesy and politeness are regarded as standard' (independent preparatory school head-teacher, Buckinghamshire).

These views come from independent preparatory schools, play-groups, infant schools and special schools, and may indicate the ideologies found in these settings which set them apart from the day nurseries and nursery schools. In the latter settings the influence of a nursing ethos and a Rousseau-derived belief in the innate, uncorrupted, goodness of the infant may be averse to the strict training and civilizing of the 'young savages' approach. Training for conformity appears to permeate those settings where children are 'getting ready' for the next stage of formal schooling.

Major stories – people and relationships

We have grouped together a cluster of themes which are concerned with people and relationships in early years settings. This 'people' aspect of a quality curriculum covers such issues as special needs, class size, social interactive learning, the role of parents and the training and qualities of staff. The practitioners we surveyed are clear and unequivocal in linking quality in the early years with highly trained and appropriately specialized staff who receive, as an entitlement, further in-service training, and this reinforces the findings we recorded in earlier chapters. The appropriate training for teachers is perceived as requiring graduate status and that of other staff as at least of NNEB level. All early years staff are expected to be 'specialists' in their field and particularly well trained in child development. The phrases which often occur are 'in-depth knowledge' and 'thorough knowledge' of child development, or, an understanding of 'how children learn'. Many respondents also express a need for further in-service training which is frequent and meaningful, while being an easily accessed entitlement for all early years workers.

It is also apparent that the appropriate initial training and ongoing professional development of staff are not sufficient of themselves, they must be matched with special qualities and attitudes. The key words in this respect are 'caring', 'sharing', and 'receptive'. 'Caring' is used to identify the practitioner's approach to young children and early years education; 'sharing' is usually about knowledge, practice and the learning experience; and 'receptive' hints at a stance towards professional training and expertise, as well as towards what can be learned from young children and their families.

One respondent succinctly voices the main themes of staff training, qualities and attitudes: 'Quality education depends on *qualified* caring staff who are specifically trained for early years, guiding and supporting and making valuable key interactions' (nursery school headteacher, London).

The notion of 'valuable key interactions' in this response derives from an influential cognitive psychology story which has come to dominate the latter half of the twentieth century. Learning of a particularly rapid and effective kind occurs when child and adult are in partnership and solve problems together. The source of this story is Vygotsky (1978) and the metaphor he developed of a 'zone' of potential development which can be traversed by the child in the course of sharing tasks with a tutoring adult. Such key interactions effectively make the child 'a head taller' (*op. cit.*, p. 102) in achievement terms and this has become a central metaphor in modern early years education. It is a view of learning which can be linked to the earlier discussion of 'environment' in that an appropriate early years learning environment is frequently characterized as full of 'opportunities','caring', 'happy and safe', 'comfortable', 'welcoming', 'secure', 'organized' and 'well-resourced'.

Every type of setting surveyed, although not every individual institution, produced some comments on 'parents', sometimes seeing them as a source of help in the classroom, but most frequently as the other partners in the early education enterprise. This partnership metaphor focused on the knowledge parents have of their own children and the need for practitioners to tap into such a rich resource. A quality curriculum, we were frequently told, is 'One which allows the partnership between the practitioner and parents to develop in order to share knowledge of their children's experience, skills and abilities' (special school headteacher, Hampshire).

This professional picking of brains can be a rather one-sided model of a partnership but a few respondents have a more reciprocal understanding of the knowledge and learning which are rooted in homes and communities: 'Children come to school with a variety of experiences and an already increasing understanding of their environment and the world around them and that learning does not come in neat little bundles' (infant school headteacher, Norfolk). The metaphor at the end of this comment is a vivid reminder of the resistance from some early years workers to an imposed National Curriculum which can, and must, be 'delivered' in discrete subject packages (neat little bundles).

Major stories – planning, records, assessment

Relatively few respondents in the nursery and primary settings voice explicit objections to the National Curriculum and its programme of assessment on the grounds of its inappropriateness for the early years, unlike those playgroup leaders whose thoughts on both of these we quoted in Chapter 3. All the sectors, however, express a strong commitment to appropriate planning, record keeping and assessment, so that the story which emerges is an implicit indictment of approaches to curriculum which are focused on summative tests and arbitrary 'standards'. The practitioners refer to rigorous record keeping and ongoing assessment as 'tools' for future planning and learning of a highly individual kind. As part of a quality curriculum, the assessment of children's progress is effected through observations made and carefully recorded and reflected on by trained staff: 'Rigorous record keeping systems, including sampling of children's work, to build a profile of individual children's learning . . . also used to plan for individual and group needs' (nursery school headteacher, London). A belief in informative record keeping which celebrates what young children can do and informs further planning comes through in this data.

Minor stories

A handful of minor stories occurring in the data are of interest because of the perspectives they afford on some, or all, of the range of settings surveyed.

One such story is a tale of silent refusers and a few courteous apologizers in every setting (plus one irate infant school response which effectively created a 'get lost' category). It was a mere handful of respondents who apologized for not answering Question 19 – 'How would you describe a quality curriculum for young children?' – citing lack of time: 'I don't have the time to write this – so much has been already written' (nursery school headteacher, Cambridgeshire) – or pressure of work: 'Regretfully I must decline to respond to this question, not through choice but through pressure of work' (independent preparatory school headteacher, Hampshire).

But the silent majority of this minor group left the question blank and together the blanks and the apologies total 111 out of our 542 returned questionnaires. The distribution of nil returns to the quality curriculum question indicates a high level from primary schools (31), followed by play groups (19), independent preparatory schools (16) and infant schools (15). Most of these 'refusals' are blanks and we can only hazard a guess that the pressures of the National Curriculum in terms of subjects and the related testing and inspection procedures may account for the high primary school figure. This reason might also account for the infant school blanks but the playgroups and independent preparatory schools do not fit easily into this hypothesis and other reasons have to be sought. Granted that many independent schools do follow the National Curriculum fairly closely and are inspected, it may still be the case that some of those surveyed found the question irrelevant or daunting. Some playgroups may associate the term 'curriculum' with the syllabus found in the compulsory stages of schooling and perceive our question, as we saw in Chapter 3, as irrelevant to their non-statutory settings.

We have also grouped another minor theme with the tale of the silent refusers and polite apologizers: it is the 'attached document without comment' response. In these instances (27) a document is attached, without a commentary, to Question 19. The documents include local authority curriculum guidelines, guidelines from particular institutions, the 'vision statement' of some settings, brochures, syllabuses and photo-copied quotations from early years publications and 'experts'. Only day nurseries and playgroups did not respond in this way. Perhaps this indicates that many of these settings lack written curriculum guidelines and, again, do not see 'curriculum' as a central issue for documentation.

There are questions which arise about the uncritical use of documents in an apparent avoidance of engaging at an individual professional level with the issue of a quality early years curriculum. Is this in fact evidence of another 'porky pie' of self-deception when it comes to shaping the early years curriculum? Is it symptomatic of a surrender to the busy daily routine in early years settings, having thought once in the past about formulating curriculum guidelines, or left it to others to do so? Is it a sign that practitioners either accept being told what to do, or believe that continual rethinking of curriculum issues is unnecessary?

In contrast to the silences and evasions of the stories discussed above, a very small number of practitioners articulated their views about the early years curriculum in terms of passionately held 'beliefs'. We named these minor stories 'credo' and were reminded that all narrative theories identify stories about belief systems and ideals as central functions of narrative. Such stories articulate and clarify the tellers' values: 'We believe each child should enjoy and benefit from nursery as it is the foundation of their school life' (nursery school headteacher, Berkshire). 'I firmly believe in childhood and that McMillan and Isaacs hold the core ideals' (nursery school headteacher, North Yorkshire).

If the blanks and evasions discussed previously were 'porky pies', these explicit belief statements must be a form of 'Just So' stories. They are only found in a few nursery school responses and serve as a reminder that this sector of early years provision is grounded in a strongly articulated philosophy of social improvement and 'rescue' for children and their carers.

There was other evidence of core ideals which centred on the significance of early years education as a positive foundation for later schooling and life. Once again this is highest in the responses from nursery schools and tends to reflect the optimism of the romantic movement with a stress on the dawn of life and starting with a lasting glow. Many references to creating an ideal indoor and outdoor learning environment are based on the notion of a secluded garden for children in which adults protect, stimulate and nurture children's all-round growth and development.

We might conclude that these are some of the shaping metaphors of early childhood care and education. The next step in a deeper analysis would involve identifying and collating the metaphors which pervade these stories from early years practitioners. Something of this kind has been done by Cortazzi (1991) for primary teachers, based on his interviews with 123 of them. He was able to identify and analyse 96 narratives about primary children's 'breakthroughs' in learning in terms of 'clicks', 'lights' and 'movement' (*op. cit.*, p. 127). Of course primary teachers are a more homogeneous and easily identified professional group than the wide spectrum of early years practitioners in England and Wales! But what hidden and overt metaphors, or clusters of metaphors, can be found in the range of responses we received? Although we have not, as yet, tackled this analysis formally, the following three clusters suggest themselves as starting-points: 'positive power', 'space' and 'structure'.

Metaphors

Positive power

The responses to our invitation to describe a quality curriculum for the early years contain many references to the 'life-affirming' nature of quality. Behind this idea there seems to lurk a metaphor about a positive charge of power, as in electricity, which drives the enterprise and leads to the following words and phases:

> enabling; warm; stimulating; relaxed; enrichment; comfortable; opportunities; co-operation; potential; dynamic interface between children and adults; nurture interactions; involved with children's family/community; focus on self-esteem; value individual independence; centred on child

The hidden metaphor of a positive power surge is hinted at in the words for warmth, comfort and nurture, as well as in the references to dynamics, stimulus and potential. There are also words which hint at channelling and managing power, as in 'focus' and 'centred'. Positive power is behind the many references to 'the life' of a school, nursery or other setting and leads to what may be described as a hedonistic cluster of life-affirming references:

> happy; fun, fun-loving; joy, enjoyment; pleasure; exciting; enthusiasm; celebrating; love of learning; joy of learning; attitudes to learning; a daily adventure for the learner

These remarkably up-beat clusters, suggest a positive and joyous approach to educating and caring for young children which may be a distinguishing characteristic of early years practitioners. The final overt metaphor, above, of the young child setting out on an adventure every day has always pervaded children's literature and folk stories and is found in the writings of many education pioneers. Perhaps this is a defining metaphor of early years culture.

Space

If the 'daily adventure' is a defining metaphor another important one is 'space' . The notion of space is often expressed as the traditional garden space and can be found in several cultural traditions as the paradise garden. In modern usage it is linked with a space for growth and development inside secure boundaries: a kind of safe 'playground' setting for play and explorations. All these ideas about a special type of space created for young children are implicated in the following words and phrases:

> grow; flourish; context; broad boundaries; wide range of opportunities/experiences; plenty of leeway; wide spectrum of learning

The last two phrases provide, respectively, a nautical allusion to calm, protected, space and a term from physics which implies the full range and breadth of any phenomenon.

Another cluster of words and metaphors are focused on what young children can do and be in their safe garden-playground:

> play; first-hand experience; imagination; explore – going places; choice; investigations; creative; experiments; spontaneity; inquisitive; curiosity; free activity; opportunities; challenges

The frequent use of topographical terms makes it clear that this space metaphor permeates educational thinking and planning:

> levels of functioning; levels of development; areas of learning; inside space/learning environment; outside space/learning environment

References to 'inside/outside' are a reminder that there are both literal and deeply metaphorical notions of space, gardens and playgrounds pervading early years culture. The work of Winnicott (1971) proposes a potential space which comes into being between infant and carer and is filled with emotionally significant objects like soft toys, favourite blankets and even thumb-sucking and nose-stroking. Later, this site, or third area of experiencing, is filled with playing and, later still, the rich cultural and social experiences of adulthood.

Difficult and deep metaphors of this psychoanalytical kind may inform the thinking of some practitioners and enter the folk psychology of early years practice. Respondents do refer to the importance of young children's personal space and private time:

> reflective; value privacy; time, quality time; time to develop play; space to be alone and space to organize events

It is noteworthy that this concept of a curriculum which allows for time to stand and stare still survives among early years practitioners, despite the current pressures and influences which tend to promote the busy rather than the reflective approach.

Structure

Early years practitioners' traditional respect for space and individual growth is not incompatible with a strong sense of the significance of structure in education. An awareness of the curriculum as a structure which is, in effect, one of the shaping powers of a culture pervades the responses. As does a clear sense that it is the responsibility of the adult worker to build, or create, this structured learning environment:

- adult responsibility
- created environment
- stable, safe, secure, caring
- caring environment
- colourful, rich, stimulating, broad, balanced, depth

The curriculum provides a set of holding forms, or a framework, for representing experience and this is expressed in such terms as:

> a framework; flexible; structure but not rigidity; a gentle structure

The learning environment must be built on proper foundations:

- sound base/sound foundations
- firm foundations
- strong foundations
- lays groundwork

But this is not like making a totally fresh start because, ideally, we can use the materials which the children and their families provide:

- an extension of the home
- extending children's learning
- access to children's strengths
- bridges between home and school
- stretching the child
- tailored to meet children's needs

This group of metaphors includes several from the building trade, as in 'extensions', 'access' and 'bridges', but there is also that worryingly popular notion of the child 'on the rack' and being stretched – like human elastic! The final metaphor in this group suggests that we can 'sew' the appropriate learning environment, rather than build it, thus ensuring a bespoke curriculum for every young child, perhaps.

There remains, however, a strong sense that the structure of the quality curriculum must be built:

- building on earlier skills and knowledge
- building on previous learning
- building on children's strengths
- building on what the child can do
- build opportunities

Yet it is the one biological metaphor in the responses which sums up the importance of early years learning settings: they are the 'backbone of the curriculum'.

These stories, then, as our analysis shows, confirm the view we expressed at the outset that in educational research counting is not enough. Certainly the narrative model which we have employed, eclectic in essence but drawn largely from a literary tradition, has enabled us to begin to get beyond the surface level of the quantitative data and reach deeper strata of understandings.

They also reveal, however, that even the stories themselves are not enough. For they need to be seen against a moral landscape of which they are a part.

Practitioner narratives and a moral landscape

Telling the children

Story is never enough, nor is talk. We must be told, when we are young, what rules to live by. The grownups must tell the children early in life

so that the myth and morality proclaim the same message while the
children are still listening.

(Paley, 1992, p. 110)

These words come from a book in which the habit of rejection, of some
children by their peers in the earliest days of kindergarten, is challenged
by their teacher Vivian Gussin Paley. Paley is a teacher and lifelong action researcher in her own classroom and on this occasion evolved a
mixed-methods strategy for resisting young children's arbitrary cruelty
and rejection. She combines mythic stories which parallel the classroom
situation with a simple strong rule, 'You can't say you can't play' and
uses Socratic dialogue about the rule and the myths to explore with the
children the moral landscapes of their classroom and school.

While few, if any, of our practitioners would claim to have evolved
as powerful and radical an articulation of this moral standpoint in
their early years settings, they do appear to be operating in the same
moral landscape. One respondent defines a quality curriculum for
the early years in terms which are echoed by many of our practitioners and clarify some of Paley's 'rules to live by' (above): 'It implies processes of learning in which we come to appreciate what is
valuable in human life in terms of economic viability, a just order of
social life, valued forms of personal relationships, and an ability to
communicate ideas, information and emotions' (independent preparatory school, head of junior school, Kent). The words here are all
about caring and teaching with commitment and strongly held attitudes: 'valuable', 'valued', 'human life', 'personal relationships'.
Teachers and carers are most typically engaged and committed to
telling children what they care about and value. There is, as yet, little
evidence of their switching to the technicist role of simply delivering
centrally imposed curriculum outcomes, or meeting minimal criteria
for accreditation.

This core concern with social and moral issues is a feature of our
curriculum tales. For example, a play-leader describes 'a curriculum
that helps build self-esteem' and this idea recurs in interviews with
two headteachers, one from a large inner-city primary school and one
from a large independent preparatory school in an affluent leafy sub-
urb. In the words of the latter, we must focus on 'getting the person
right in the early years'. Both heads emphasize, like all traditional
tellers of tales, the moral core of their stories, but they do so in warm
and life-affirming terms which centre on young children's happiness,
success and self-esteem. One of them rejects a curriculum which is
'pumping a child full of facts and information' and pleads for breadth
and richness through the arts and creativity. The other talks movingly
of a need to help young children to build on their obvious enthusiasm

for the world: 'Life has got to appear to them to be full of excitement and praise.' It would seem that many early years practitioners' notions of 'balance' in the curriculum are less focused on desirable outcomes and foundation subjects, and more concerned with children's social, moral and emotional growth through a rich variety of learning experiences which engage them fully.

A concern for the moral and social curriculum is articulated in these narratives and identified by respondents as 'absolutely essential'. Many of the teacher practitioners tell about establishing classroom rules, order and group dynamics, but a broad range of other practitioners also identify the needs of very young children coming into a group setting for the first time, in terms of care and personal attention. In the words of an infant teacher, 'some need to have a special personal relationship with the teacher; they can't be happy until they know that you know them somehow'. Special school practitioners were very aware that the curriculum was about individual children's learning and their partnership with a carer-teacher: 'the centre of the curriculum is the learner – actively seeking out new experiences – and the adult working with and learning about the child. '

Telling ourselves

The processes of teaching and learning are interactive and social and the roles of learners and teachers are frequently interchangeable. We who are the professional teachers, carers and instructors are frequently learning as much as we are teaching, if not more. Similarly, as narrators we need to tell ourselves our stories and work on understanding them. So, the stories we tell the children and the stories we tell about our work with children have the potential to change our lives and our professional practice.

This is, of course, the strong argument for focusing on practitioner narratives as one crucial element in the research described in this book. Other research, in different cultures and with older children as the focus, agrees with our claim that the teacher, or other responsible adult in a group setting, is the ultimate key to educational change and improvement (Huberman, 1993). But the latter research also supports our findings that professionals do not look to in-service education for remedying their own shortcomings, preferring individual and informal strategies, or, 'a swarm of private experiments' (*op. cit.*, p. 256). We might point to the swarm of private experiments now being generated by our research project and take this as a powerful definition of action research. Huberman also noted that the Swiss teachers in his project were deeply grateful for the opportunity to reflect deeply on

their lives and work through narrative exchanges with their colleagues – and to do this seriously.

These kinds of interpretive exchanges are what we take to be central
to narrative and can lead to changes which transform individuals and
institutions. Studies of the development of professional critical awareness, again undertaken with teachers in many countries, highlight the
ways in which reflection promotes self-knowledge and self-
determination (Diamond, 1991). In our next and final chapter we will
explain in greater detail how important insights of this kind led us to
adopt an action research approach to professional development in our
quest for quality. For we are persuaded that the sharing of narrative
exchanges is central to genuine professional development. Perhaps it
is that the power of this kind of self-telling frees us from the passive
victim role and lets us tell emancipatory stories about what care and
education could be like, if we wanted it enough.

This brief account of the narratives produced by respondents to the
first part of the PiP research project creates a context for our developing understanding of the mass of data already collected. It also sets the
scene for the many stories currently being told by the action researchers who are working with us in a range of early years settings.
The next set of PiP narratives will come from them as they conduct
their swarm of private experiments and quietly change their worlds: 'I
pin my hopes to quiet processes and small circles in which I believe I
shall see, if I'm still alive at the end, vital and transforming events
taking place' (Britton, 1981, p. 10). Such transforming stories are worth
waiting for.

5

The quest for quality: the action research approach

All educators would claim that quality in education is of paramount importance. As we have seen in the stories reported in the previous chapter, however, opinions differ as to the nature of this quality and the processes by which it can be promoted and developed. Earlier sections of this book have provided the practitioners' view of what quality early education entails – their guiding principles of good practice. This final section addresses the second key issue in the debate about quality – the processes by which quality can be achieved. In doing so, it provides the link between the principles and the practice of quality early years education.

It thus leads us into the second phase of the project – dissemination and development. This phase is still at an early stage, and this section will seek merely to offer some preliminary understandings gained from our pilot studies. A subsequent publication will develop the story at greater length when we are somewhat further down this road.

The challenge facing the project team at the start of Phase Two, the developmental stage of the work, was to find an appropriate means by which practitioners might ensure that their principles of quality provision were effective in practice. Initially, the team considered the various strategies offered by the school effectiveness movement (Reid et al., 1987) to address the issue of improving the quality of education. These strategies were assessed and evaluated in terms of their potential for effecting real improvement in the daily practice of those practitioners directly responsible for working with young children along the lines dictated by their conception of quality provision. Those strategies, however, appeared to be managerial in essence and thus unlikely to lead to an enhancement of quality as this is envisaged by practitioners in the field.

As earlier chapters will have indicated, we have found that a more personal approach, one which empowers the practitioner by offering scope for taking ownership of his or her own professional practice, appears to be more effective, certainly in the early years sector. As was argued in Chapter 4, a personal and interpersonal approach and one which offers practitioners ample opportunities to take on the role of spectators in their professional lives seemed more appropriate. For this spectator role entails the making of stories, reflecting critically and creatively on these stories and sharing them with colleagues in a supportive professional context. And this is a process which aims to give space and time for reflection on the full implications of what often turn out to be muddled ideas or myths, and to reconstruct more useful and genuinely 'true to experience' hypotheses to explain and guide professional practice. An action research strategy was ultimately selected, therefore, since this appeared to fulfil these criteria.

There are varying definitions and descriptions of action research but the general consensus appears to be that it is a process of self-reflective inquiry by practitioners into their own practice in order to improve that practice. The approach adopted by the project team aims to encourage practitioners to look beyond the managerial and operational concerns of their practice, not merely concentrating on ensuring things are achieved in the most productive ways or evaluating pupils' learning simply in terms of their end results, but extending their evaluations to the whole learning experience. This is intended to be a more holistic process that will include an appraisal of an activity's value as well as the role the practitioner might play within it.

In this approach, when practitioners undertake action research, they decide upon a specific area of their own practice they wish to investigate and improve upon. They then gather information about this aspect of their practice in order to increase their knowledge and deepen their understanding of the issue in question.

A useful way of beginning this process is to consider their existing views of the area under focus and then to spend some time reviewing what is actually happening, usually by observation. In one pilot study, for example, practitioners chose to look at the teacher's role in developing reading (Edwards and Rose, 1994). In this study, it proved necessary for the action researchers to clarify what they believed that role should be before gathering evidence about it from their own practice. In looking more closely at their chosen focus, they collected evidence in a variety of ways. They asked colleagues to observe them reading with a child or they tape-recorded reading sessions. Or they simply observed children reading. Practitioners will invariably select a variety of means by which to find out more about their practice, providing a variety of perspectives from which to review it.

The next step is perhaps the most crucial part of the action research process and requires the practitioners to reflect critically upon the data gathered. In asking probing questions and deliberating on any new findings, practitioners can then take active steps to adjust their practice to accommodate the insights gained from their observations. Once these changes have been introduced, the practitioners continue to observe and reflect in a continuous cycle of professional development and improvement.

In this way, our pilot studies provided us with a range of practical understandings and principles upon which to plan and implement Phase Two of the project, in which members of the project team worked alongside the practitioners as research partners, giving them information and advice where necessary and often assisting with the collection and evaluation of the data gathered. Our next section highlights the principles that guided the project team and led to the selection of action research as a strategy for enabling practitioners to improve the quality of their practice.

Why was action research adopted?

In the same way that practitioners are guided by fundamental principles about the most appropriate way to conduct their practice, the project team identified several conditions which it considered to be necessary for promoting educational quality. An attempt has been made by the team to provide a rationale for these guiding principles and a clarification of the reasons why action research is seen as offering the most effective strategy for addressing the issue of quality in education.

The key to quality lies with the practitioner

The school effectiveness movement has endeavoured to identify those factors which appear to be influential in developing so-called 'good schools'. Reid *et al.* (1987), for example, cite factors such as clear goals, consistent policies, well planned lessons and monitoring systems. These factors may well play an important part in ensuring an effective educational environment. However, the PiP team is committed to the view that the key to achieving quality lies with the practitioners themselves. Any attempts to bring about improvements in education, therefore, ought to focus attention fundamentally upon the practitioner and his or her practice, and all other considerations or solutions should be recognized as hingeing on this central factor. Indeed, in their review of the wealth of research into school effectiveness, Reid *et al.* (*op. cit.*, p. 30) state that 'the quality of the teaching staff is perhaps the single most important factor'. A government paper has likewise acknowledged that 'the teaching force . . . is that major single determinant of the quality of education' (DES, 1983, p. 1). And in our project survey, as we saw in earlier chapters, heads of early years institutions have cited the qualities of staff as a crucial factor for ensuring quality in practice.

Action research was chosen as our strategy, then, because it not only focuses attention on the practitioner's actual practice but it also stimulates practitioners themselves actively to evaluate the quality of their practice. It is critical, self-evaluative inquiry that enables practitioners to consider the context of their practice. While conducting action research, practitioners are called to question particular aspects of their practice, to articulate the underlying values and assumptions which inform and influence that practice, and to consider the effectiveness of their professional actions and judgements, especially in the light of the impact these have on the children with whom they work. Whilst policies and plans may play their part, the team believes that it is the practitioners' self-awareness of their day-to-day activities and decisions that is most influential in effecting quality practice. Closer observation of practice helps practitioners to deepen their understanding of children's learning. This then enables them to make better evaluations and more appropriate decisions about learning experiences. And this in turn improves the quality of their provision. It is a process which bridges the gap between theory and practice and broadens and deepens professional understanding, not just of educational knowledge but of their professional role within it.

Educational improvement requires the professionalism of practitioners

If practitioners are the key to effecting quality, they need to be empowered to respond to the challenge of improving their practice. The PiP team suggests that, for strategies to have any real chance of success, practitioners need to feel that their sense of professionalism is being enhanced, particularly in a climate in which teacher professionalism has been eroded by recent legislation (Gilroy, 1991). The inevitable consequence of a tightly prescribed National Curriculum, linked with highly bureaucratic systems of assessment and inspection, is that teachers act primarily as interpreters and implementers of external directives. Moreover, policies such as the management-led teacher appraisal system, and evaluation of nursery education by reference to 'desirable outcomes', effectively become an official monitoring system which can act more as a threat to the practitioners than as a means to self-improvement. They are unlikely to develop honest self-criticism in a situation in which they feel judged, especially when the criteria of judgement are at odds with their own professional principles, nor are their motivation and morale likely to be increased in such circumstances. Stenhouse (1975, p. 143) has highlighted that it is 'not enough that teachers' work should be studied; they need to study it themselves'. And he added that 'we do not enable people to jump higher by setting the bar higher, but by enabling them to criticize their present performance' (*op. cit.*, p. 83).

Action research embraces a practitioner's professional judgement, and, in doing so, it is a means by which practitioners may regain their professional identity. A context is being created in which professional judgement is given priority over simplistic skills and where deliberation replaces rule-following (Grundy, 1989). The deeply questioning process of action research demands that practitioners query every aspect of their practice, including their educational judgements. The vigorous questioning of personal assumptions, together with the collaborative nature of action research, helps to guard against misguided practice and some of the potential dangers of poor teacher judgement. As Elliott (1991, p. 52) puts it, action research 'improves practice by developing the practitioner's capacity for discrimination and judgement in particular, complex, human situations . . . informing professional judgement'. Through action research, practitioners develop their 'practical wisdom' (*ibid.*). The development of such 'practical wisdom' can help practitioners to make more appropriate judgements.

The value of action research, then, is that it gives credence to practitioners' professional judgement as well as encouraging them to take fulfilment from and control of their practice. This in turn can help to re-enthuse and re-empower practitioners to confront the challenge of improving their practice and becoming willing participants and initiators of beneficial change.

Imposed change is not effective

Most of the changes currently taking place in the name of improving educational quality are imposed from above. This top-down approach, in which all changes are centrally dictated, controlled and managed, may not be the most effective way of reforming educational provision. A number of writers have noted the evidence that a centrally dictated system, with little scope for individuality and flexibility, achieves minimal success (Holt, 1987; Kelly, 1989). And the now-defunct Schools Council eventually realized that attempts to introduce innovations from outside the school proved ineffective, and this led to the adoption of a new approach which encouraged school-based curriculum development (Kelly, 1990). Nor is this surprising, since practitioners will 'resist changes that do not make sense to them' (Heckman, 1987, p. 67). And, in like fashion, Fullan (1982) notes the need for practitioners to find meaning in and for change. And so, 'for effective learning to take place teachers need to feel in control of change rather than to feel controlled by change' (Blenkin, Edwards and Kelly, 1992, p. 55).

Graham (1993) writes that 'the best and most effective change comes from within', and action research enables practitioners to transform their practice in a safe, supportive and self-directed environment. Since changes are self-initiated, the impact is likely to have a more genuine effect. And so the team adopted the strategy of action research because of the way in which it gives practitioners control of developments so that they become meaningfully convinced of the changes which need to take place to improve their practice.

Education is a process not a product

With the advent of the National Curriculum, attention has become focused on the achievement of fixed outcomes. As we have seen in earlier chapters, our evidence indicates that this shift of emphasis from the 'how' to the 'what' of education is regarded as misdirected by many early years practitioners. From the research team's perspective, educational achievement, especially in early childhood, should be defined in terms of a continuous process of striving rather than of a fixed and finite attainment. In the same way that Fullan (1982) notes that change is a process not an event, so this is true of the development of educational understanding. If children are to be helped in their capacity for learning, educators need to concentrate their energies on how to support this progress if the goal is to be achieved effectively. It is a question of deliberation on the means and not merely on the ends. The team was thus drawn to action research as providing a practical way for practitioners to engage in this kind of deliberation on the processes of learning.

Educational practice is complex, unpredictable and ambiguous

Many of the government initiatives and the school effectiveness approaches imply that teaching is a stable activity which can be made more precise, predictable, efficient and cost-effective through the application of certain techniques or rules. It is assumed that the knowledge and skills which underpin successful teaching can be precisely stated and that performance can be measured against specific, standardized competencies. Acknowledgement needs to be made, however, of the fact that, since education involves humans and not machines, it is not possible to predict conveniently or to program its results. Grundy (1989), for example, makes the crucial point that practitioners can never be sure that their choice of activity will provide a meaningful and beneficial learning experience for every child, not least because every learning experience is unique to each child. She compares the teacher's uncertainty about educational outcomes with the way in which no judge can be sure that sentencing will be just retribution for a crime. Fullan (1993, p. 45) agrees, saying that 'teaching is intrinsically and perennially an uncertain profession'. In this context, quality cannot become a predetermined product but must be an ongoing process.

Action research is flexible and adaptable, and it accommodates itself to the particular needs and circumstances of each practitioner and his or her practice. Not only does it acknowledge the complexity, unpredictability and ambiguities of educational practice, it is also itself a ceaseless process. It is a strategy which precludes the imposition of any formal or rigid structure or programme, and recognizes that the 'context of practice is always changing and requires continuous innovation' (Elliott, 1985, p. 504). The project team was thus attracted by the capacity of action research to accommodate itself to any context and to provide practitioners with a practical tool capable of responding appropriately to the challenges and uncertainties of educational practice.

Collaborative practice ensures quality for all children

Whilst action research is self-directed, it also enables practitioners to extend their professional practice through collaborative processes, helping to counteract the isolationist tendencies which have sometimes characterized the education profession. For, although the focus is on self-reflection, this can be done within a collaborative context, embracing both the individualism and the collectivism which Fullan (1993) maintains are crucial for effective change. Since action research must operate in a context of mutual trust and co-operation, the team believed that practitioners would feel less intimidated about disclosing personal fears and uncertainties. Further, the supportive structure of action research can encourage practitioners to take risks and to develop a 'collaborative culture' (Lieberman and Miller, 1990).

This focus for professional collaboration helps to stimulate mutual debates about what is happening in practice and the value of it. Such co-operative practice enhances the provision for the children and helps to ensure that their educational experiences are consistent and of equal benefit to all.

This, then was the thinking which led the team to select this form of action research as the strategy which it felt was likely to be most effective in supporting the kinds of professional development it was seeking to promote in Phase Two.

The action research pilot studies

Once the strategy of action research had been adopted, the project team sought the co-operation of various institutions which cater for young children aged 0–8. Staff in eleven settings in the London area agreed to participate in the pilot phase of the project. Three others were invited but declined. The eleven participating settings included a range of early years provision in both the private and the maintained sectors, with representation from day nurseries, nursery schools, infant and primary schools. The participants themselves came from a range of professional backgrounds and held varying levels of responsibility within their institutions, from nursery nurses to headteachers.

Developments within the case studies

As with all case study material, it is difficult to draw clear distinctions which appropriately reflect the developments within each setting. The particular attributes which influenced and affected the process of each individual action research project were often relevant only to the context of each individual setting. Attempts to identify meaningful patterns, therefore, have been made very carefully. The team judged each pilot study on the basis of its own merit and then sought to identify some key aspects of the ways in which the action research appears to have affected the different practitioners in their practice. These different aspects were then reviewed and key features, along with some commonalities of experience, were drawn out to gain a more collective picture of the ways in which action research can enhance the quality of educational provision.

The conclusions which are offered here, therefore, are those which were made to assist the project team as it undertook the main phase of its action research studies. This is currently in progress and will be the subject of a further publication of findings.

The analysis is based on a range of material which includes reports and field notes made by research partners after each visit, as well as action research evidence collected by both the research team and the individual practitioners involved. These data for the most part involved written observations of children and adults and audio and video material. The evaluations were made by the action researchers themselves, although this was often done in conjunction with members of the research team, the research partners with whom they were working. Finally, the data included reflective journals written by some of the action researchers and some transcribed tape-recordings of action research meetings between members of the project team and the action researchers. The research team also met on several occasions during the year to discuss and compare developments within each setting.

Of the eleven settings which participated, at least seven were deemed to have made worthwhile progress. The nature of that progress is of course a matter for debate and clearly one of the most critical issues in any research analysis.

The project team, therefore, drew up a number of conditions or 'success criteria' which enabled the team to reach considered decisions concerning the effectiveness of action research as a strategy for professional development. The most important criterion of all was the reports made by the action researchers themselves, where the practitioners themselves reported benefits and improvements in their practice as a direct result of the action research study. These reports were then compared with the research partner's evaluation of the developments within the case study based on the evidence available to them, including their own field notes. In a majority of cases, a decision by the setting to continue the project beyond the pilot year was also regarded as an important factor in evaluating its effectiveness. Detailed accounts of three of the more successful case studies can be found elsewhere (Blenkin and Paffard, 1994; Boorman, 1994; Edwards and Rose, 1994).

It is clear from the more successful case studies that action research helped the practitioners to recognize and appreciate more of what was happening in their practice. This increased awareness often led the participants to re-evaluate appropriate practice and it also opened up possible alternatives. One of the most valuable gains was the confirmation or recognition of the need to use close observation as a diagnostic tool and of the need to be more analytical in assessing the quality of what children do. For observations carried out often revealed different explanations of what was happening in practice and raised new questions about and insights into children's learning. Indeed, some of the practitioners were conscious of advances in their thinking, and others reported the ways in which the action research had challenged previously held assumptions about their practice. There were also comments about the fact that action research had rekindled an interest in children's learning and had improved their sense of professionalism. This was described by some as feeling 'more accountable' for what they were doing, and they felt more able to explain and justify it.

The level of involvement of other members of staff varied according to the type of setting, but there were many examples of colleagues not directly involved expressing a critical and supportive interest in the research, and this provided a valuable focus for professional collaboration. It is also worth noting that involvement in the action research brought some practitioners to a realization of the relevance of research and its applicability to their own practice, so that they ceased to view it as something undertaken by academics and thus of no consequence to them.

The other four settings did not satisfy the 'success criteria' for a variety of reasons. However, even the reasons for a lack of development provided the project team with a number of valuable insights into some of the difficulties which can be encountered when conducting action research. We conclude by detailing some of the lessons thus learned.

Lessons learned

Perhaps the most significant aspect of the pilot study was that each setting created many different learning opportunities for the research partners to take with them into the next main phase of the project. And from these studies it was possible to identify a range of factors deemed significant for promoting the process of professional development through action research. Conversely, the research partners were also able to distinguish a number of features which appeared to inhibit such progress. Thus, in the review of the case studies, a series of factors became apparent which could be related to every case setting.

These factors included the participating practitioners' personal motivation and their confidence in their practice. For example, in those settings where the participants did not appear to be personally committed to undertake the action research, little development took place. This is illustrated by the case of one of the participating primary schools. Here the main action researcher was a Key Stage 1 teacher who had joined the pilot project at the request of her headteacher. It gradually became clear that this teacher considered the work a 'chore'. In contrast, the reception and nursery teachers became involved and expressed more interest, so that soon they took the initiative. These two teachers are still developing their work in the main action research phase of the project and have made some significant improvements in their practice, particularly in relation to the links between nursery and reception and smoothing the path for children as they change classes. In comparison with the Key Stage 1 teacher, these early years practitioners displayed a determined commitment to action research that was personally motivated, and this clearly paid off in terms of their own professional development.

Similarly, the confidence of the practitioner and the ability to take ownership of his or her own professional development was a common feature which emerged from those case studies where the researchers were deemed to have benefited from the action research. In contrast, at least two of the less successful settings appeared to have been either inhibited by the presence of academic staff or cautious about making their practice 'public'. It may be of some significance that these two case settings were in the private sector. For example, in a preparatory school concerns were expressed about the impact of the action research on the parents; whilst in a private day care nursery members of the staff team were unwilling to undertake their own observations and preferred to let the research partner take the lead. They appeared to view the action research as a passive training session rather than as an opportunity to develop their own practice in a meaningful way. These examples can be contrasted with another setting in which a group of reception teachers were quite undaunted by the academic status of the project. In this setting the participants also had the personal self-assurance to investigate their practice and to confront the risks involved in exposing possible inadequacies.

It is also worth noting that most of the case studies deemed by the team to be more successful at the pilot stage were undertaken by teaching staff. The background and training of the practitioner may therefore be of significance in relation to the impact of action research strategies. On the other hand, this judgement may reflect the values of the research team, most of whom were themselves qualified teachers.

It must be noted, however, that one of the most successful pilot case studies was the work of a nursery nurse. Her careful study of young babies has helped her to make some important changes in her practice. This includes the resourcing and reorganization of the setting as well as developing her understanding of the adult role. Her continued work in the project is evidence that this practitioner has the confidence to take action to improve the quality of her practice and has taken clear control of her own professional development.

The practitioners who made the most progress were those who were able to take control themselves of the direction of their action research and to undertake their own observations in parallel with appropriate evaluations. The act of conducting observations and subsequent reflection on these observations ensured that the practitioners were directly affected by their findings and able to adapt their everyday practice accordingly. Their capacity to take the lead in their own professional development is the most rewarding and far-reaching effect of the action research.

However, not all practitioners were confident or committed enough to do this right away. In at least four of the more successful settings, the research partners had to begin by working sensitively with the practitioners to build up their confidence, and sometimes they had to model and guide the observations before the practitioners began to take the initiative and ultimately regulate the action research themselves.

An additional issue which became apparent was that of working with groups. In the majority of settings the research partners worked with individuals. This was considered to be preferable in order to ensure a sense of personal ownership and personal impact. Indeed, one of the settings which did not develop effectively was one involving a group of six practitioners. The research partner felt that this indicated that a group of this size was too large to be effective. In another pilot study, which involved several practitioners, differences began to arise between those responsible for the various age-groups. Factors such as this appeared to prevent the action research process from moving forward.

A common sense of purpose appears to be necessary if practitioners working together are to develop their practice and, within this, the critical factor of personal involvement arises again. In the setting where tensions arose between the age-groups, the action research only began to take off when the Key Stage 1 staff withdrew and left the nursery and reception teachers working towards a shared goal. Likewise, in one of the infant schools, three reception teachers effectively carried out the action research together. The fact that they already worked together as team in this five-form entry school undoubtedly helped the group dynamics to work to their advantage.

However, the complications of working with groups of practitioners and the significance of the need for personal motivation and commitment led the project team to focus mainly on working with individuals when it entered the main action research phase of its work.

This issue of individual versus group work, however, merits further exploration. For, while at the level of the individual settings it seems clear that action research by individuals is more likely to be effective, there is a growing and quite striking body of evidence emerging of the advantages to be gained from creating opportunities for those individuals to meet regularly to 'compare notes' with others pursuing their own action research in different settings. And regular 'conferences' of action researchers and the project team have become an increasingly significant feature of the work as it has progressed.

There remains much more to be learned about the merits, the advantages and the pitfalls of action research as a strategy for promoting the professional development of practitioners working in the early years of education. Our research so far has revealed most clearly both that there is much need for such development and that it is crucial to the achievement of high-quality provision in this sector.

In Phase Two of the project, therefore, with the support of number of local authorities, and on the basis of what we have learned from the pilot study described here, we are extending our action research activities to a greater range of settings. Our purposes in this are twofold. First, and centrally, we see this as a necessary extension of the project's work into the field of dissemination and development. For the intention is both to support the continuous professional development of selected practitioners working in this sector, and, while doing so, to encourage as many others as possible to recognize the value of action research for their own professional development and to engage in it individually and collectively.

Second, however, we are at the same time seeking to monitor and evaluate the processes of action research itself. We are keen to identify the optimum conditions for it to be effective and to discover the more serious barriers to its effectiveness. For it is our belief, as we hope we have made clear, that school effectiveness in the early years must be evaluated by reference to more than simplistic learning outcomes, and that, on our definition of effectiveness, the quality of the practitioner is the most important factor in ensuring the quality of the provision.

It is becoming increasingly clear that policies for early education are crucial to the future of the nation, both economically and socially. There is thus much attention currently being devoted to those policies. If, as a nation, we are to get them right, we need as full an understanding as can be achieved of what constitutes the right kind of educational provision for young children and of preparation for the adults who work with them.

This research is seeking to make its own contribution to the combined tasks of establishing what is a quality curriculum for the early years and assisting practitioners to provide it for all children as effectively as possible.

We hope that this book demonstrates that we have already learned much. As Phase Two proceeds we hope to learn much more. This we will report in a subsequent publication. In the mean time, the message is 'watch this space'.

Appendices

A   Standard guidelines for structured interviews

GOLDSMITHS' COLLEGE, UNIVERSITY OF LONDON

FACULTY OF EDUCATION

Early Childhood Education Research Project

"Principles into Practice"

Improving the Quality of Children's Early Learning

INTRODUCTORY EXPLANATION : We wish to reassure you the starred (*) questions which require detailed answers can be answered more fully on our separate document which can be filled in at your leisure.

INTERVIEW FOR HEAD OF EDUCATIONAL INSTITUTION OR GROUP, AND OTHER PARTICIPANTS

1   Name of Interviewer and Name of Interviewee, Time, Date, Place.

2   Name and Address of Educational Institution or Group

3   What is the Financial Status of Your Institution: Independent, Voluntary, Local Authority, Funded by Employer, etc.?

*4   The children Under-8 on Roll

   A   What are your numbers, including any part-time, approximately?

   B   What are the ages of the under-8s catered for?

   C   How many other languages are spoken by the children in your institution?

   D   What are your policies and approaches to children with Special Needs? [If interviewee requests definition of SN] In your institution how do you identify children with Special Needs, apart from those formally designated so for you?

E   Do most of the children travel for more or less than 30 minutes from home?

If appropriate:

F   How are the children organised, are they in groups based on age or any other form of grouping? What size are the groups?

G   What kind of work are parents involved in?

*5   Staffing

A   What is the staff/child ratio?

B   What are the different roles of staff, i.e. teacher, nursery worker, cook, etc.?

C   What are the qualifications of staff, e.g. courses and qualifications such as BEd., PGCE, QTS, GCSE, City and Guilds, Nursing Diplomas, NVQs, etc.?

D   How do staff work, i.e. in teams, singly, etc.?

6   The Premises

A   Who owns or provides the premises [e.g. employer, education authority, council, church, hospital, etc.]?

B   Who maintains the premises?

C   Brief description of surroundings [i.e. city centre, industrial estate, suburbs]

D   Number and size of rooms available.

E   How do you use the rooms, e.g. classroom, parent's room, cloakroom, playroom, staff room, extended day provision, etc.?

F   Outdoor playspace, resources and fixed equipment [e.g. playground, field, garden].

7   **Aims of the Educational Institution or Group**

Either
A(i)   Do you have a printed statement for parents about what you intend the curriculum to be?

Or
A(ii)   What are the main features of your prospectus and how were they decided upon?

B   Do you have a printed statement or statements about what the curriculum should be for the use of staff?

If appropriate:

C   If employer-funded, do you have a statement of your aims for your employer?

D   How are decisions taken about the weekly and daily activities provided?

E   Are there any sources of ideas and information that you find helpful in your work with under-8s?

F   During the last year has any member of staff participated in further training, In-Service Education, or other professional development and support?

G   What do you think is the value of these activities?

8   **Records and Assessment**

A   What records do you keep on individual children?

B   What formal assessment do you use with your under-8s?

C   Do you keep any other kind of written records?

D   How do you record the daily activities provided for individuals and/or groups of children?

9   Parents

A   To what extent do you have contact with the parents?

B   Do you ever meet parents to discuss their children's progress?

C   Do you have any policies on relations with parents or projects involving them?

10   How Would You Describe a Quality Curriculum for Young Children? [A written response would be welcomed.]

Thank you for your help!

Geva Blenkin, Vicky Hurst and Marian Whitehead
Early Childhood Education Research Project: "Principles into Practice"

[For ECERP Office only:

Date received: .... Ref no: ....]

GOLDSMITHS' COLLEGE, UNIVERSITY OF LONDON
FACULTY OF EDUCATION

Early Childhood Education Research Project

PRINCIPLES INTO PRACTICE: Improving the Quality of Children's Early Learning

---

In most countries in the world, the importance of early learning is increasingly being recognised and attempts are being made to improve the quality of provision for children from birth to eight years of age. It is in this context that the Early Childhood Education Project at Goldsmiths' College has been established. This questionnaire is designed both to gather information about current provision for children at this important stage in their education and to glean the opinions of you and your colleagues in relation to potential areas for development. Its main purpose is to create a base of understandings from which improvements might be planned. Your cooperation in completing the questionnaire is thus very important, and by doing so you will be contributing directly to that process of development.

We appreciate your cooperation. We would also point out that data gathered in this questionnaire will be treated confidentially and presented only in summary form without the name or the affiliation of the respondent.

Name of respondent: ....

Status: ....

Name and address of educational institution or group:

....

....

....

....

Telephone number: ....

Age range of children catered for: ....

B　National survey questionnaire

Part I: Information Related to the Institution

1 Of what type is your institution/group? (Please tick as appropriate)

Nursery school	[ ]1	Nursery class	[ ]7
Infant school	[ ]2	Workplace nursery	[ ]8
First school	[ ]3	Independent preparatory school	[ ]9
Primary or JMI	[ ]4	Independent nursery school	[ ]10
(Junior mixed and infants)			
Local authority day nursery	[ ]5	Playgroup	[ ]11
Private day nursery	[ ]6	Special needs school/unit	[ ]12

Others, please specify: ....

2 Status of your institution/group: (Please tick as appropriate)

Independent	[ ]1	Grant Maintained	[ ]4
Local Authority	[ ]2	Funded by Employer	[ ]5
Voluntary	[ ]3	Others, please specify:..................................	

3 Does your institution share accommodation with other institution(s)/group(s)?

Yes　[ ]1　　　　　　　　No　[ ]2

If Yes, please specify: ....

4 Please give a brief description of the surrounding environment? (Please tick as appropriate)

Inner city	[ ]1	Traditional rural area	[ ]4
Urban area	[ ]2	Commuter rural area	[ ]5
Suburban area	[ ]3	Mixed area	[ ]6

Others　　[ ]7　　Please specify: ....

5 Do the children have access to outdoor play space at your institution/group?

Yes　[ ]1　　　　　　　　No　[ ]2

If Yes, what is the style of access? (Please tick as appropriate)

Continuous	[ ]1
Occasional	[ ]2
Infrequent (eg requires an expedition with adults, supervised playtime etc.)	[ ]3

6 Number of full-time and part-time children on roll in each age group: (Please state the number of children in each age group)

Age:	0	1	2	3	4	5	6	7	8	For BCERP office only: Total
Full-time	[ ]	[ ]	[ ]	[ ]	[ ]	[ ]	[ ]	[ ]	[ ]	[ ]
Part-time	[ ]	[ ]	[ ]	[ ]	[ ]	[ ]	[ ]	[ ]	[ ]	[ ]

7 Gender of children in each age group: (Please state the number of boys and girls in each age group)

Age:	0	1	2	3	4	5	6	7	8	For BCERP office only: Total
Boys	[ ]	[ ]	[ ]	[ ]	[ ]	[ ]	[ ]	[ ]	[ ]	[ ]
Girls	[ ]	[ ]	[ ]	[ ]	[ ]	[ ]	[ ]	[ ]	[ ]	[ ]

8 Number of children with English as a second language (ESL) in each age group: (Please state the number of ESL children in each age group)

Age:	0	1	2	3	4	5	6	7	8	For BCERP office only: Total
Children whose first language is not English (ESL)	[ ]	[ ]	[ ]	[ ]	[ ]	[ ]	[ ]	[ ]	[ ]	[ ]

Part II: Number & Qualifications of Staff

9 What is/are your own qualification(s)? (Please tick as appropriate)

BA(Ed)/BEd/B.Add	[ ]1	BTech	[ ]8	PPA Diploma in Playgroup Practice	[ ]14
BA	[ ]2	MA/MEd/M.Add	[ ]9	PPA Tutor & Fieldwork Course	[ ]15
BSc	[ ]3	Cert.Ed.(2 years)	[ ]10	PPA Further Course	[ ]16
NNEB, City & Guilds or equivalent	[ ]4	Cert.Ed.(3 years)	[ ]11	MPhil/PhD	[ ]17
		Montessori Certificate	[ ]12	None	[ ]18
SRN	[ ]5	PPA Short Courses	[ ]13	Others, please specify:	[ ]19
PGCE	[ ]6	e.g. Learning Through			
NVQS	[ ]7	Play, First Aid etc.			

....

10 Please indicate the number of full-time and part-time staff, both paid and voluntary, who work closely with children under-8 (including yourself if appropriate).

Full-time paid	[ ]1	Part-time paid	[ ]3
Full-time voluntary	[ ]2	Part-time voluntary	[ ]4

11 What are the qualifications of the staff (other than yourself) who work closely with children under-8? (Please state numbers for each gender in each category)

	Teachers (1)	Support teachers (2)	Nursery nurses (3)	Nursery workers (4)	Classroom assistants (5)	Others (6)
Q1 BA(Ed)/BEd/B.Add						
Male	[ ]1m	[ ]2m	[ ]3m	[ ]4m	[ ]5m	[ ]6m
Female	[ ]1f	[ ]2f	[ ]3f	[ ]4f	[ ]5f	[ ]6f
Q2 BA						
Male	[ ]1m	[ ]2m	[ ]3m	[ ]4m	[ ]5m	[ ]6m
Female	[ ]1f	[ ]2f	[ ]3f	[ ]4f	[ ]5f	[ ]6f
Q3 BSc						
Male	[ ]1m	[ ]2m	[ ]3m	[ ]4m	[ ]5m	[ ]6m
Female	[ ]1f	[ ]2f	[ ]3f	[ ]4f	[ ]5f	[ ]6f
Q4 NNEB, City & Guilds or equivalent						
Male	[ ]1m	[ ]2m	[ ]3m	[ ]4m	[ ]5m	[ ]6m
Female	[ ]1f	[ ]2f	[ ]3f	[ ]4f	[ ]5f	[ ]6f
Q5 SRN						
Male	[ ]1m	[ ]2m	[ ]3m	[ ]4m	[ ]5m	[ ]6m
Female	[ ]1f	[ ]2f	[ ]3f	[ ]4f	[ ]5f	[ ]6f
Q6 PGCE						
Male	[ ]1m	[ ]2m	[ ]3m	[ ]4m	[ ]5m	[ ]6m
Female	[ ]1f	[ ]2f	[ ]3f	[ ]4f	[ ]5f	[ ]6f
Q7 NVQs						
Male	[ ]1m	[ ]2m	[ ]3m	[ ]4m	[ ]5m	[ ]6m
Female	[ ]1f	[ ]2f	[ ]3f	[ ]4f	[ ]5f	[ ]6f
Q8 MA/MEd/M.Add						
Male	[ ]1m	[ ]2m	[ ]3m	[ ]4m	[ ]5m	[ ]6m
Female	[ ]1f	[ ]2f	[ ]3f	[ ]4f	[ ]5f	[ ]6f
Q9 MPhil/PhD						
Male	[ ]1m	[ ]2m	[ ]3m	[ ]4m	[ ]5m	[ ]6m
Female	[ ]1f	[ ]2f	[ ]3f	[ ]4f	[ ]5f	[ ]6f
Q10 BTech						
Male	[ ]1m	[ ]2m	[ ]3m	[ ]4m	[ ]5m	[ ]6m
Female	[ ]1f	[ ]2f	[ ]3f	[ ]4f	[ ]5f	[ ]6f
Q11 Cert.Ed. (2 years)						
Male	[ ]1m	[ ]2m	[ ]3m	[ ]4m	[ ]5m	[ ]6m
Female	[ ]1f	[ ]2f	[ ]3f	[ ]4f	[ ]5f	[ ]6f
Q12 Cert.Ed. (3 years)						
Male	[ ]1m	[ ]2m	[ ]3m	[ ]4m	[ ]5m	[ ]6m
Female	[ ]1f	[ ]2f	[ ]3f	[ ]4f	[ ]5f	[ ]6f
Q13 Montessori Certificate						
Male	[ ]1m	[ ]2m	[ ]3m	[ ]4m	[ ]5m	[ ]6m
Female	[ ]1f	[ ]2f	[ ]3f	[ ]4f	[ ]5f	[ ]6f

	Teachers	Support teachers	Nursery nurses	Nursery workers	Classroom assistants	Others
	(1)	(2)	(3)	(4)	(5)	(6)

Q14 PPA Diploma in
    Playgroup Practice

Male	[ ]1m	[ ]2m	[ ]3m	[ ]4m	[ ]5m	[ ]6m
Female	[ ]1f	[ ]2f	[ ]3f	[ ]4f	[ ]5f	[ ]6f

Q15 PPA Tutor & Fieldwork
    Course

Male	[ ]1m	[ ]2m	[ ]3m	[ ]4m	[ ]5m	[ ]6m
Female	[ ]1f	[ ]2f	[ ]3f	[ ]4f	[ ]5f	[ ]6f

Q16 PPA Short Courses
    e.g. Learning Through
    Play, First Aid etc.

Male	[ ]1m	[ ]2m	[ ]3m	[ ]4m	[ ]5m	[ ]6m
Female	[ ]1f	[ ]2f	[ ]3f	[ ]4f	[ ]5f	[ ]6f

Q17 PPA Further Course

Male	[ ]1m	[ ]2m	[ ]3m	[ ]4m	[ ]5m	[ ]6m
Female	[ ]1f	[ ]2f	[ ]3f	[ ]4f	[ ]5f	[ ]6f

Q18 None

Male	[ ]1m	[ ]2m	[ ]3m	[ ]4m	[ ]5m	[ ]6m
Female	[ ]1f	[ ]2f	[ ]3f	[ ]4f	[ ]5f	[ ]6f

Q19 Others,
    Please specify:

    ....

Male	[ ]1m	[ ]2m	[ ]3m	[ ]4m	[ ]5m	[ ]6m
Female	[ ]1f	[ ]2f	[ ]3f	[ ]4f	[ ]5f	[ ]6f

12 Where individual members of staff are counted more than once in question 11, please indicate their gender, role and their combination of qualifications.
Examples: female teacher - BA(Ed), MA
                male nursery nurse - NNEB, SRN
(Please use additional sheets if necessary)

13 Have any of your staff re-trained for work with children under-8? (Please state numbers for each gender in each category)

	Early Years Age Range			
	0-3 (1)	0-5 (2)	5-8 (3)	3-8 (4)
S1 BA(Ed)/BEd/B.Add				
Male	[ ]1m	[ ]2m	[ ]3m	[ ]4m
Female	[ ]1f	[ ]2f	[ ]3f	[ ]4f
S2 BA				
Male	[ ]1m	[ ]2m	[ ]3m	[ ]4m
Female	[ ]1f	[ ]2f	[ ]3f	[ ]4f
S3 BSc				
Male	[ ]1m	[ ]2m	[ ]3m	[ ]4m
Female	[ ]1f	[ ]2f	[ ]3f	[ ]4f
S4 NNEB, City & Guilds or other equivalent				
Male	[ ]1m	[ ]2m	[ ]3m	[ ]4m
Female	[ ]1f	[ ]2f	[ ]3f	[ ]4f
S5 SRN				
Male	[ ]1m	[ ]2m	[ ]3m	[ ]4m
Female	[ ]1f	[ ]2f	[ ]3f	[ ]4f
S6 PGCE				
Male	[ ]1m	[ ]2m	[ ]3m	[ ]4m
Female	[ ]1f	[ ]2f	[ ]3f	[ ]4f
S7 NVQs				
Male	[ ]1m	[ ]2m	[ ]3m	[ ]4m
Female	[ ]1f	[ ]2f	[ ]3f	[ ]4f
S8 BTech				
Male	[ ]1m	[ ]2m	[ ]3m	[ ]4m
Female	[ ]1f	[ ]2f	[ ]3f	[ ]4f
S9 Cert.Ed.				
Male	[ ]1m	[ ]2m	[ ]3m	[ ]4m
Female	[ ]1f	[ ]2f	[ ]3f	[ ]4f
S10 Montessori Certificate				
Male	[ ]1m	[ ]2m	[ ]3m	[ ]4m
Female	[ ]1f	[ ]2f	[ ]3f	[ ]4f
S11 PPA Diploma in Playgroup Practice				
Male	[ ]1m	[ ]2m	[ ]3m	[ ]4m
Female	[ ]1f	[ ]2f	[ ]3f	[ ]4f
S12 PPA Tutor & Fieldwork Course				
Male	[ ]1m	[ ]2m	[ ]3m	[ ]4m
Female	[ ]1f	[ ]2f	[ ]3f	[ ]4f
S13 PPA Short Courses e.g. Learning Through Play, First Aid etc.				
Male	[ ]1m	[ ]2m	[ ]3m	[ ]4m
Female	[ ]1f	[ ]2f	[ ]3f	[ ]4f
S14 PPA Further Course				
Male	[ ]1m	[ ]2m	[ ]3m	[ ]4m
Female	[ ]1f	[ ]2f	[ ]3f	[ ]4f
S15 Others, please specify:				
....				
Male	[ ]1m	[ ]2m	[ ]3m	[ ]4m
Female	[ ]1f	[ ]2f	[ ]3f	[ ]4f

14 If you have Qualified Teachers on your staff, which age range were they trained for initially? (Please state numbers for each gender in each category)

				Age Range				
	3-5 (1)	3-8 (2)	5-7 (3)	3-11 (4)	5-11 (5)	7-11 (6)	11-16 (7)	Others (8)

Qualified Teacher Status:

R1 BA(Ed)/BEd/B.Add

Male	[ ]1m	[ ]2m	[ ]3m	[ ]4m	[ ]5m	[ ]6m	[ ]7m	[ ]8m
Female	[ ]1f	[ ]2f	[ ]3f	[ ]4f	[ ]5f	[ ]6f	[ ]7f	[ ]8f

R2 PGCE

Male	[ ]1m	[ ]2m	[ ]3m	[ ]4m	[ ]5m	[ ]6m	[ ]7m	[ ]8m
Female	[ ]1f	[ ]2f	[ ]3f	[ ]4f	[ ]5f	[ ]6f	[ ]7f	[ ]8f

R3 Cert.Ed

Male	[ ]1m	[ ]2m	[ ]3m	[ ]4m	[ ]5m	[ ]6m	[ ]7m	[ ]8m
Female	[ ]1f	[ ]2f	[ ]3f	[ ]4f	[ ]5f	[ ]6f	[ ]7f	[ ]8f

R4 Others, please specify:

....

Male	[ ]1m	[ ]2m	[ ]3m	[ ]4m	[ ]5m	[ ]6m	[ ]7m	[ ]8m
Female	[ ]1f	[ ]2f	[ ]3f	[ ]4f	[ ]5f	[ ]6f	[ ]7f	[ ]8f

15 Have any of your qualified teachers engaged in further study related to early childhood education? (Please state numbers for each gender in each category)

	In-service BEd (1)	Professional Diploma (2)	MA/MEd/ M.Add (3)	MPhil/PhD (4)
Male	[ ]1m	[ ]2m	[ ]3m	[ ]4m
Female	[ ]1f	[ ]2f	[ ]3f	[ ]4f

Others, please specify:

.... [ ]male [ ]female

.... [ ]male [ ]female

.... [ ]male [ ]female

Part III: The Quality of Early Learning

Please note that in this section we are asking for your general views on the quality of early learning, regardless of your own institution/group.

16 **The following list identifies some of the factors that support the development of an appropriate curriculum for young children. Please tick the FIVE that you consider to be the MOST significant factors.**

Qualifications of staff [ ]1

Range of experience of staff [ ]2

Length of experience of staff [ ]3

Qualities of staff [ ]4

Provision for staff development and INSET [ ]5

Evaluating provision [ ]6

Keeping records of children's learning [ ]7

Assessment of children [ ]8

Effective partnership with parents [ ]9

High ratio of staff to children [ ]10

Provision of an effective environment for learning [ ]11

An adequate physical environment for learning [ ]12

A supportive social environment [ ]13

High quality resources for early learning [ ]14

Adequate number of resources for early learning [ ]15

Management structure of the institution/group [ ]16

Others, please specify:

....[ ]

....[ ]

....[ ]

....[ ]

....[ ]

17 **The following list identifies some of the factors that constrain the development of an appropriate curriculum for young children. Please tick the FIVE that you consider to be the MOST constraining factors.**

Staff not trained for early years specialism   [   ]1

Inexperienced staff   [   ]2

Inadequate levels of staffing   [   ]3

Lack of opportunities for staff training and INSET   [   ]4

Poor monitoring of provision   [   ]5

Inappropriate procedures for assessing children   [   ]6

Inadequate provision for parental involvement   [   ]7

Restricted space for learning   [   ]8

Inappropriate accommodation   [   ]9

Limited opportunities for learning out of doors   [   ]10

Insufficient budget for resources   [   ]11

Poor management of the institution   [   ]12

Others, please specify:

.... [   ]

.... [   ]

.... [   ]

.... [   ]

.... [   ]

18 **What factors do you think are influential in the professional development of practitioners working with children under-8?** (Please place a "1" against the most influential factor and a "2" against the next most influential factor and so on. For two or more factors which you think are of equal importance, please place the same number against each factor)

Knowledge of child development   [ ]1

Meticulous planning   [ ]2

Organisational skills   [ ]3

Knowledge of school subjects   [ ]4

Ability to assess individual children   [ ]5

Feedback from staff appraisal   [ ]6

Regular staff meetings   [ ]7

Partnership with parents   [ ]8

Openness to change   [ ]9

Understanding of educational issues   [ ]10

Familiarity with recent research   [ ]11

Access to professional journals   [ ]12

School based in-service training   [ ]13

Local Authority based in-service training   [ ]14

Higher Education based in-service training   [ ]15

19 **How would you describe a quality curriculum for young children?**
(Please use additional sheets if necessary)

20 What improvements would you like to see in the current educational provision for under-8s and in the professional training and development for practitioners who work with young children?   (Please use additional sheets if necessary)

Improvements on current educational provision for under-8s:

Improvements on professional training and development for practitioners who work with young children:

Thank you very much for completing this questionnaire.

Would you be available for further discussions/interviews?   Yes   [ ]1   No   [ ]2

Please return the questionnaire to:

Dr Nora Y L Yue
Early Childhood Education Research Centre
Faculty of Education
Goldsmiths' College
University of London
New Cross, London SE14 6NW

C   Justification of the methodology used in the determination of the sample size for the survey

It is evident that an increase in sample size will lead to an increase in the precision of the sample mean as an estimator of the population mean. However, the sampling costs will also increase and there is likely to be some limit on what we can afford. Too large a sample will imply a waste of resources; whereas too small a sample is likely to produce an estimator of inadequate precision. Ideally we should state the precision we require, or the maximum cost which we can expend, and choose the sample size accordingly.

Such an aim involves a complex array of considerations:

- What is the cost structure for sampling in a given situation?
- How do we assess the precision we require of our estimators?
- How do we balance needs in relation to *different* population characteristics which may be of interest?
- How do we deal with a lack of knowledge about the parameters (e.g. the population variance) which may affect the precision of estimators?

It is the last consideration that we are most concerned about in our particular study. In this survey, the main population characteristic in which we are interested is:

- The nature and qualifications of practitioners working with children under 8.

There has been no previous research which seeks to identify this characteristic in the population of practitioners working with children under 8 in England and Wales. There is no record, therefore, of the population variance which could be used to estimate the required sample size for our survey.

In addition to this, there is a range of different institutional settings in which the practitioners are working with children under 8, and there has been no previous measurement of variability on the nature of the qualifications of practitioners within each of these settings. We needed, therefore, to find alternative ways of estimating the required sample size which would represent both the whole population and a valid sample from each of the types of provision. And we needed to do this without prior knowledge of any measurement of variability within this population.

There are basically four ways in which we might have set about the task of estimating the minimum sample size required when the population variance S^2 is unknown.

From pilot studies

If the pilot study itself takes the form of a simple random sample, its results may give some indication of the value of S^2 for use in the choice of the sample size of the main survey.

The selection of participants in our pilot study does not take the form of a simple random sample since it was made through contacts. Therefore, if the pilot sample is not obtained by a probability sampling procedure, we must be circumspect in such an application of the results. In addition, the pilot study is often restricted to some limited part of the population, and so the estimate of S^2 which it yields for the population characteristic can be quite biased.

From previous surveys

It is not uncommon to find that other surveys have been conducted elsewhere which have studied similar characteristics in similar populations. Often the measure of variability from earlier surveys can be used to estimate S^2 for the present population, in order to choose the required sample size to validate any prescription of precision in the current work. However, the characteristics we have chosen to study in this survey have not been explored elsewhere previously. Hence, we have no previous measurements of variability from which we could estimate the sample size required for our survey. Furthermore, taking measurements from previous studies may also introduce error, and precautions must be taken in extrapolating measurements from one situation to another.

From a preliminary sample

This is the most reliable approach. However, it was not feasible on administration and cost considerations for our project. This approach operates as follows. A preliminary simple random sample of size n_1 is taken and used to estimate S^2 by means of the sample variance s_1^2. We aim to ensure that n_1 is inadequate to achieve the required precision, and then to augment the sample with a further simple random sample of size $(n-n_1)$, where $(n-n_1)$ is chosen by using S_1^2 as the necessary preliminary estimate of S^2. The total sample size needs to be

$$(1+2/n_1)s_1^2/V$$
(where V = variance of the sample mean)

an essential increase by the factor $(1+2/n_1)$ over what would be needed if S^2 were known.

This approach, if feasible, is undoubtedly the most objective and reliable. This sampling procedure is known as *double (or two-phase) sampling.*

From practical considerations of the structure of the population

Occasionally we will have some knowledge of the structure of the population which throws light on the value of S^2. In these cases, there is reason to believe that the Y-values (the measurements of characteristics from each sample of the population) might vary roughly in the manner of a Poisson distribution, so it is plausible to assume that S^2, is of the same order of magnitude as the population mean. Any information we have about the possible value of the population mean (e.g. from other similar studies) can then be used to estimate S^2 and assist in the choice of the required sample size. Furthermore, if we can assume that S^2 = population mean, then we can obtain an approximate $100(1-\alpha)\%$ symmetric two-sided confidence interval for the population mean directly, without the need for an estimate of variability.

In our survey, we were interested in estimating a proportion of the population having a certain characteristic. In this case, the sampling variance of the simple random sample estimator is simply related to the population proportion. The procedure used in determining our sample size for estimating the true population proportion is explained in detail below.

The task of determining the size of the sample needed requires prior specification of the desired level of confidence and the acceptable margin of error between the values of $\overline{X}$ (the sample mean) and μ (the population mean). The margin of error, or error of estimate is often called the error tolerance to reflect the imprecision a decision-maker is willing to tolerate. The margin of error E is specified as the absolute value of the difference between the point estimate $\hat{p}$ and the true population proportion p; it is written as

$$|\hat{p}-p| = E$$

The expression for determining the sample size requires the value of E, the value of $Z_{\alpha/2}$ (determined from the level of confidence specified) and an initial estimate of p, denoted by p^*:

$$n = (Z_{\alpha/2} / E)^2 p^*(1-p^*)$$

Prior to sampling, available information about p based on past experience or theoretical considerations may be used as a base for the specified value for p^*. If, prior to sampling, there is no reasonable basis for specifying p^* (which is the case in this survey since there has been no previous study), then p^* is set to 0.5. In the latter case, we use $p^* = 0.5$

because it can be shown that the product $p^*(1 - p^*)$ reaches a maximum value of 0.25 when $p^* = 0.5$. When $p^*(1 - p^*)$ is set at 0.25, the above equation maximizes the value for n, the needed sample size, thereby assuring that the margin of error will be within the specified range with at least the specified level of confidence, no matter what the actual value of p. If the numerical value for n found from the above equation is not an integer, the result is rounded up to guarantee that the confidence level will be at least $1 - \alpha$. Table A shows the maximum sample size required for estimating p for various confidence levels.

Table A   Sample size (no. of institutions) required for estimating the true population proportion

| | Confidence level | | | |
| | 99% | 98% | 95% | 90% |
Margin of error (%)				
2	4,148	3,382	2,401	1,692
5	664	542	385	271
6	461	376	267	188
7	339	276	196	138
8	260	212	150	106
10	166	136	97	68

The sample size for the questionnaire survey was determined according to the sample population for each type of under-8s provision and the funding available. The latter was crucial in determining the survey sample size.

It was decided that for each type of under-8s provision, in order to claim, with at least 90% confidence, that the observed value of the sample proportion is within 7% of the true proportion of each type of provision, a random sample of 138 institutions/groups was needed for each type of provision (see Table A – 90% confidence level, 7% margin of error).

Since in all questionnaire surveys it is almost impossible to obtain 100% response, it is necessary to adjust and compensate the sample size required for the survey. It was anticipated that in this survey we would expect a response from at least half of our targeted institutions/groups. Therefore, the sample size chosen for each type of provisions was $2 \times 138 = 276$. Provisions with sample population less than 276 were surveyed in full.

The methodology used in selecting the survey sample is known as two-stage cluster sampling with unequal cluster sizes (a simple random sample of education authorities, and a simple random sample of under-8s provisions under each of the selected authorities).

D   Principles into Practice Steering Committee

Phase One membership

Chair
Professor A.V. Kelly (Professor of Curriculum Studies, Goldsmiths' College)

Project Director
Ms Geva Blenkin

Deputy Directors
Ms Marian Whitehead (School Settings)
Ms Victoria Hurst (Preschool Settings)

Representative of National Interests in Early Education
Baroness Mary Warnock

Representative of Associated Projects
Professor Kathy Silva (RSA Early Childhood Project)

Representative of National Children's Bureau
Dr Gillian Pugh (Early Childhood Unit Director)

Representative of a Local Education Authority
Ms Linda Pound (Early Years Inspector, London Borough of Greenwich)

Headteacher of a Statutory Age School for Early Years Pupils
Mr John Meehan (Mayflower Primary School)

Headteacher of a Nursery School
Ms Francis Marriott (Rachel McMillan Nursery School)

Representative of Non-School Early Years Provision
Ms Kate Docherty (Head of Early Years Service, London Borough of Lewisham)

References

Adelman, C. (ed.) (1977) *Uttering, Muttering: Collecting, Using and Reporting Talk for Social and Educational Research*, Grant McIntyre, London.

Audit Commission (1996) *Counting to Five*, Audit Commission, London.

Ball, S.J. and Goodson, I.F. (eds.) (1985) *Teachers' Lives and Careers*, Falmer, Lewes.

Barrett, G. (1986) *Starting School: An Evaluation of the Experience*, AMMA and Centre for Applied Research in Education, Norwich.

Bennett, M. (ed.) (1993) *The Child as Psychologist*, Harvester Wheatsheaf, Hemel Hempstead.

Blenkin, G.M., Edwards, G. and Kelly, A.V. (1992) *Change and the Curriculum*, Paul Chapman, London.

Blenkin, G.M., Hurst, V.M., Whitehead, M.R. and Yue, N.Y.L. (1995) *Early Childhood Education Research Project, Principles into Practice: Improving the Quality of Children's Early Learning, Phase One Report*, Goldsmiths' College, University of London.

Blenkin, G.M. and Kelly, A.V. (eds.) (1996) *Early Childhood Education: A Developmental Curriculum* (second edition), Paul Chapman, London (first published in 1987).

Blenkin, G.M. and Paffard, F. (1994) Telling Verona's story, *Early Years*, Vol. 15, no. 1, pp. 30–36.

Blenkin, G.M. and Yue, N. (1994) Profiling early years practitioners; some first impressions from a national survey, *Early Years*, Vol. 15, no. 1, pp. 13–22.

Blum-Kulka, S. (1993) You gotta know how to tell a story, *Language in Society*, Vol. 22, pp. 361–402.

Board of Education (1931) *Primary Education* (the Hadow Report), HMSO, London.

Boorman, P. (1994) A question of balance: principles and practicalities in physical education, *Early Years*, Vol. 15, no. 1, pp. 48–53.

Britton, B.K. and Pellegrini, A.D. (eds.) (1990) *Narrative Thought and Narrative Language*, Lawrence Erlbaum Associates, Hillsdale, NJ.

Britton, J. (1981) English teaching: retrospect and prospect, *English in Education*, Vol. 15, no. 2, pp. 1–10.

Britton, J. (1992) *Language and Learning*, Penguin Books, Harmondsworth.

Bruner, J.S. (1976) Nature and uses of immaturity, in Bruner *et al.* (eds.) (1976) *op. cit.*, pp. 28–64.

Bruner, J.S. (1990) *Acts of Meaning*, Harvard University Press, Cambridge, Mass.

Bruner, J.S., Jolly, A. and Sylva, K. (eds.) (1976) *Play – Its Role in Development and Evolution*, Penguin Books, Harmondsworth.

Chafe, W. (1990) Some things that narratives tell us about the mind, in Britton and Pellegrini (eds.) (1990) *op. cit., pp.* 79–98.

Cortazzi, M. (1991) *Primary Teaching, How It Is – A Narrative Account*, David Fulton, London.

Cortazzi, M. (1993) *Narrative Analysis*, Falmer, London.

Cortazzi, M. (1994) Narrative analysis, *Language Teaching*, Vol. 27, no. 3, pp. 157–70.

Davies, P. (1994) *Pre-school education: Implementation of the Voucher Scheme*, Response to Welsh Office Consultation, Children in Wales, Early Childhood Unit, Cardiff.

Department of Education and Science (1972) *Education: A Framework for Expansion* (a white paper) (Cmnd 5174), HMSO, London.

Department of Education and Science (1977) *Curriculum 11–16*, HMSO, London.

Department of Education and Science (1983) *Teaching Quality*, Cmnd 8836 HMSO, London.

Department of Education and Science (1985) *The Curriculum from 5 to 16*, *Curriculum Matters 2*, HMSO, London.

Department of Health (1991) *The Children Act 1989: Guidance and Regulations, Volume 2, Day Care and Educational Provision for Young Children*, HMSO, London.

Department of Health and Social Security/Department of Education and Science (1976) *Low Cost Day Provision for the Under-Fives* (Papers from a conference held in January 1976), HMSO, London.

Diamond, C.T.P. (1991) *Teacher Education as Transformation*, Open University Press, Milton Keynes.

Early Years Curriculum Group (EYCG) (1992) *First Things First. Educating Young Children: A Guide for Parents and Governors*, Madeleine Lindley, Oldham.

Early Years Curriculum Group (EYCG) (1995) *Four-Year-Olds in School: Myths and Realities*, Madeleine Lindley, Oldham.

Edwards, G. and Rose, J. (1994) Promoting a quality curriculum in the early years through action research: a case study, *Early Years*, Vol. 15, no. 1, pp. 42–7.

Eisner, E.W. (1985) *The Art of Educational Evaluation: A Personal View*, Falmer, London.

Elliott, J. (1985) Teachers as Researchers' in Husen, T. & Postlethwaite T.N. (eds), *The International Encyclopaedia of Education*, 9, Oxford: Pergamon Press.

Elliott, J. (1991) *Action Research for Educational Change*, Open University Press, Milton Keynes.

Feynman, R.P. (1988) *What Do You Care What Other People Think?*, Unwin Hyman, London.

Fox, C. (1993) *At the Very Edge of the Forest: the Influence of Literature on Story and Narrative by Children*, Cassell, London.

Frank, A. (1954) *The Diary of Anne Frank*, Pan, London.

Fullan, M. (1982) *The Meaning of Educational Change*, OISE Press, Toronto.

Fullan, M. (1993) *Change Forces: Probing the Depths of Educational Reform*, London: Falmer Press.

Gilroy, D.P. (1991) The Loss of Professional Autonomy: the relevance of Olaga Matyash's paper to the brave new world of British education, *Journal of Education for Teaching*, 17.1, 11–15.

Goldschmied, E. and Jackson, S. (1994) *People Under Three*, Routledge, London.

Graham, D. with Tytler, D. (1993) *A Lesson for Us All: The Making of the National Curriculum*, Routledge, London.

Gregory, R.L. (1977) Psychology: towards a science of fiction, in Meek *et al.* (eds.) (1977) *op. cit.*, pp. 393–98.

Grumet, M.R. (1990) Voice: the search for a feminine rhetoric for educational studies, *Cambridge Journal of Education*, Vol. 20, no. 2, pp. 277–82.

Grundy, S., (1985) *Curriculum: Product or Praxis?* Falmer, London.

Gudmundsdottir, S. (1991) Story-maker, story-teller: narrative structures in curriculum, *Journal of Curriculum Studies*, Vol. 23, no. 3, pp. 207–18.

Heath, S.B. (1983) *Ways with Words*, Cambridge University Press, Cambridge.

Heckman, P. (1987) Understanding School Culture in Goodlad, J. I. (ed.). *The Ecology of School Renewal*, NSSE, Chicago.

Helm, J. (ed.) (1967) *Essays on the Verbal and Visual Arts*, University of Washington Press, Washington.

Hernstein, R.J. and Murray, C. (1994) *The Bell Curve*, The Free Press, New York.

Holt, M. (1987) *Judgement, Planning and Educational Change*, Harper and Row, London.

Huberman, M. (1993) *The Lives of Teachers*, Cassell, London.

Inner London Education Authority (1987) *The Early Years. A Curriculum for Young Children*, ILEA Learning Resource Branch, London.

Jackson, B. (1979) *Starting School*, Croom Helm, London.

Kelly, A.V. (1989) *The Curriculum: Theory and Practice* (Third edition), Paul Chapman, London.

Kelly, A.V. (1990; 1994) *The National Curriculum: A Critical Review* (updated edition 1994), Paul Chapman, London.

Kipling, R. (1902; 1986) *Just So Stories*, Macmillan, London.

Labov, W. and Valetzky, J. (1967) Narrative analysis: oral versions of personal experience, in Helm (ed.) (1967) *op. cit.*, pp. 12–44.

Liebermann, A., and Miller, I. (1990) Teacher development in professional practice schools, *Teachers College Record*, Vol. 92, no. 1, pp. 105–22.

May, H. and Middleton, S. (1995) Curriculum policy and practice: a New Zealand case study of change in early childhood 'Through the eyes of teachers', paper presented at the Froebel Institute College, Roehampton Institute, London on 11 May.

McKissack, P.C. (1986) *Flossie and the Fox*, Puffin Books, Harmondsworth.

Meek, M., Warlow, A. and Barton, G. (eds.) (1977) *The Cool Web*, Bodley Head, London.

Moss, P. and Penn, H. (1996) *Transforming Nursery Education*, Paul Chapman, London.

Nelson, K. (1989) *Narratives from the Crib*, Harvard University Press, Cambridge, Mass.

Nias, J. (1985) Reference groups in primary teaching: talking, listening, and identity, in Ball and Goodson (eds.) (1985) *op. cit.*, pp. 105–19.

Office of Her Majesty's Chief Inspector (Wales) (OHMCI) (1995) *A Survey of Provision for Under Fives in the Playgroup and Maintained Sectors in Wales*, HMSO, London.

Paley, V.G. (1992) *You Can't Say You Can't Play*, Harvard University Press, Cambridge, Mass.

Patton, M.Q. (1980) *How to Use Qualitative Methods in Evaluation*, Sage, London.

Polanyi, L. (1985) *Telling the American Story*, Ablex, Norwood, NJ.

Popper, K. (1972) *Conjectures and Refutations: the Growth of Scientific Knowledge*, Routledge & Kegan Paul, London.

PreSchool Playgroups Association (PPA) (1976) *At Work Together*, PreSchool Playgroups Association, London.

Propp, V. (1968) *The Morphology of the Folktale*, University of Texas Press, Austin, Tex.

Pugh, G. and McQuail, S. (1996) *Effective Organisation of Early Childhood Services*, National Children's Bureau, London.

Reddy, V. (1991) Playing with others' expectations; teasing and 'mucking about' in the first year, in Whiten (ed.) (1991) *op. cit.*, pp. 143–58.

Reid, K., Hopkins, D. & Holly, P. (1987) *Towards the Effective School: The problems and some solutions*, Basil Blackwell, Oxford.

Sacks, O. (1973) *Awakenings*, Duckworth, London.

School Curriculum and Assessment Authority (SCAA) (1996) *Desirable Outcomes for Children's Learning on Entering Compulsory Education*, SCAA, York.

Simons, H. (1977) Conversation piece: the practice of interviewing in case study and research, in Adelman (ed.) (1977) *op. cit.*

Stenhouse, L. (1975) *An Introduction to Curriculum Research and Development*, Heinemann, London.

Solzhenitsyn, A. (1963) *One Day in the Life of Ivan Denisovich*, Penguin Books, Harmondsworth.

Trevarthen, C. (1993) Playing into reality, *Winnicott Studies 7*, pp. 67–84.

Vygotsky, L.S. (1978) *Mind in Society*, Harvard University Press, Cambridge, Mass.

Vygotsky, L.S. (1986) *Thought and Language* (revised and edited by A. Kozulin), MIT Press, Cambridge, Mass.

Weir, R.H. (1962) *Language in the Crib*, Mouton, The Hague.

Wells, G. (1987) *The Meaning Makers: Children Learning Language and Using Language to Learn*, Hodder and Stoughton, London.

Whitehead, M.R. (1994) Stories from a research project: towards a narrative analysis of data, *Early Years*, Vol. 15, no. 1., pp. 23–9.

Whiten, A. (ed.) (1991) *Natural Theories of Mind*, Blackwell, Oxford.

Winnicott, D.W. (1971) *Playing and Reality*, Penguin Books, Harmondsworth.

Wordsworth, W. (1953) Ode, 'Intimations of Immortality from Recollections of Early Childhood' V, Oxford University Press (first published 1807).

Index